ONE
TRACK
MIND

ONE
TRACK
MIND

WHAT RUNNING 150 MILES IN A DAY CAN TEACH YOU ABOUT LIFE

MICHAEL STOCKS

REED PEAK

For Jane

In memory of Eddie

CONTENTS

PART 7: WHEN IT'S OVER

PREFACE

SATURDAY, 22:40

The sharp, searing pain in my right calf is so sudden that I'm forced to stop running immediately. *There's no coming back from this. It's out of my hands. Thank God it's over.* These thoughts are a flicker that lasts no more than a moment. Then comes the dread, a wave of anguish that extinguishes everything else. *It's all been for nothing. Eighteen months of preparation, and I've failed.*

Darkness lurks behind the glare of the stadium lights as raindrops swirl in the wind. I stand rooted to the spot.

'Are you okay, Mike?' someone calls out. I don't answer because I don't know. I try to move, just one step. My calf has completely seized up – it's solid and unyielding. I try again, hobbling one step, then two, three, ten, twenty. It begins to ease. But then, suddenly, a knife cuts through the muscle again and I come to an abrupt halt. *It's over, surely.* I feel the tears welling in my eyes. *It can't end like this.*

I have another go. The pain starts to ease and by the

time I'm at the far end of the track, I'm running with only a slight limp.

Norman, my coach, is watching my every step. He's standing in the third lane as I pass by on the inside. I don't stop to talk. It's part of the plan: don't stop for anything.

'It's my calf,' is all I say as I pass him.

Around I go, now on the straight, now on the far bend. Then I'm back, running past Norman again. Jane's there too, standing under the small gazebo at the side of the track where my crew is camped. Even now, a part of me smiles at the sight of her big puffy white coat, her 'snow cone', we call it. Her face, wrapped in a woolly hat and scarf, betrays her concern.

'It's easing,' I say, running past her almost normally.

I search my body for warning signs. My joints ache, the muscles in my legs radiate a dull pain and every now and then a sharp sciatic flash shoots across my thigh and into my ankle, making me wince. My ankles and feet protest each time my soles hit the ground, but it all feels quite normal.

Incredibly, my calf seems to be working. Perhaps it will hold up – maybe it's a spasm rather than a tear in the muscle. Everything is going to be okay after all. I'm ahead of schedule and doing what I want to do. *I wouldn't want to be anywhere else in the world.*

This tiredness is temporary. I can deal with the pain. The nausea will pass. I have ten hours of running behind me. And fourteen more to go.

INTRODUCTION

BEFORE THE STORM
THREE WEEKS TO RACE DAY

I'm an ultrarunner, and in recent times the activity has taken over much of my life. It's natural, I suppose, given what I'm trying to do, and what it will mean if I succeed. In just three weeks I will try to run more than 150 miles in twenty-four hours. I am hoping to manage around 155 miles – approximately six marathons – in one day. There are many reasons for the run, but above all else is the possibility of being selected to run for Great Britain. Every step I take beyond 150 miles will give me a greater chance of being chosen to wear the GB vest at the 24-Hour World Championships.

For a long time, the idea of running for my country seemed a distant dream. Yet now, after many years of training and racing, I have a realistic chance. I will need to produce the best performance of my life and draw on all my experience. And when I stand on the starting line, I'll be forty-nine years old.

Is it really such a good idea? The thought occurs to me as I ease my legs over the side of the bed and stand up. A wave of exhaustion begs me to lie back down, but I ignore it and start to hobble towards the door. At first my ankles refuse to flex and I make limited progress, then one of them cracks and I progress to a stiff shuffle. By the time I reach the landing, I'm buoyed by my success and feel ready to face the stairs. I place one hand on the bannister and one on the wall, and lower myself down the first step. Over the past few years I've mastered walking down these stairs without actually doing any walking. The rewards are the avoidance of spasms in my immobile calf muscles, and enviable triceps.

I developed my stair technique after an operation on my ankles a couple of years ago. Once I was off crutches, I found that even though I was able to run, walking down steps could be uncomfortable. It was a year before I was able to use the escalators on the London Underground with any confidence – their big steps were my 'gold standard' for testing my ankles. My ankles are still far from perfect and occasionally I can't walk or stand, even if I can run. I'll be cooking in the kitchen or walking down the road when a flash of pain will come from nowhere and my right ankle will give way. For a minute or two I might have to stand on the other leg or sit down, but five minutes later I'll go for a run and it will be fine. The human body is a strange and wondrous thing.

My ankles worry me a bit, but a lot else about my upcoming challenge is cause for anxiety too, not least the idea of running for twenty-four hours without stopping. In some ways, running for a long time is the easy part. Yes, it is many hours longer than I've ever run before, but the bigger challenge is to do it fast enough to cover the distance I need to run for Great Britain.

It's only recently I've been able to say those words without feeling like an imposter: *run for Great Britain*. Can people who start running in their mid-thirties have such aims without deluding themselves? In truth, I gave up any notion of running glory before my teens. I may have dreamed, but I also knew that world-beating runners did not generally lose races across the field to their classmates at school. What I didn't know then, though, is that life isn't a sprint; it's more like the endless circuits around the pitch at football practice that I never minded.

The infinite possibility that exists in childhood is easily eroded by experience. I remember the media interviews that played out in my mind before my first ever race, a 5km fun run. 'So Michael, you're eight years old, can you win the big race?' 'Yes, I can – I'm going to win.' When the big day arrived, I sprinted off, and watched as hundreds of kids disappeared up the road. I walked a lot, and there was no post-race interest from the reporters in my head. Perhaps just a single interview before the next event. 'Can you win the big race, Michael?' 'No. No, I can't.'

As a thirty-five-year-old who walked in a 10km race, I had even less hope. But somehow, the sense of possibility grew as I continued to improve as an ultrarunner. Even so, it was a while before I could more easily say out loud what I was hoping to achieve. That was at the start of the two-year training-and-racing plan that has taken me through many thousands of miles to where I am today.

The race is the Self-Transcendence 24-Hour Track Race on

a standard 400-metre all-weather athletics track in Tooting, South London. Round and round we will run, from noon on Saturday, through the afternoon, the evening and into the depths of the night, continuing as the sun rises, through the morning, until noon the next day. No one gets to the finish first or last – we start and finish together and whoever runs the furthest in that time wins.

My main concern about the track is not a fear of monotony, but the bends at each end and what so many miles of repetitive curves might do to my legs. Running around a bend places different forces on the leg as it lands and pushes off, which can over so many hours be a cause of injury.

I've made it down the stairs, across the hall and into the kitchen. As I fill the kettle, I wonder how I'm going to get through the day, let alone do any productive work. During my peak training weeks, there's an underlying fatigue that seeps into every other part of life. Yesterday's 31-mile run was the last of my longer efforts and the end of my hardest training block, which included a 50-mile run two weeks ago. Occasionally, I'm very productive the day after a long run, as if my brain is in some kind of 'hyper mode', but more often I find it difficult to concentrate.

I have my own business, so must be disciplined. It helps to know that there are international runners all around the country who find the time and energy to train every morning before heading off to work and then often again at night. Their daily lifeline is not the financial support of the athletics authorities or the National Lottery, but the patience and encouragement of partners, family, friends and colleagues.

At the centre of my own support network is my wife Jane.

She has never begrudged me the time and energy I spend training. She crews me at races, believes in me and helps me believe in myself.

When we met, in Dublin, I was a burned-out businessman living on wine, pizza, coffee and thirty cigarettes a day. As she tells the story, I was *grey*. That was certainly how I felt: physically and mentally devoid of colour. Jane saw through the grey and helped me find the colour inside.

My sister Anne and my parents are 6,000 miles away in South Africa. It's hard being so far away, but we do our best and manage to see each other a few times a year, which is more than most people in our situation. Anne has crewed me at many races and my father gives me the advice that underpins my approach to training and racing. My mother inflicts news of my races on her friends, and while I feel some sympathy for them, I also value her pride in me.

Then there is my mother-in-law, Eve. Eve has cancer and her sudden decline has been difficult to bear. She's my number-one fan and is supportive, encouraging and generous. Seeing her suffer is horrible. Almost as bad is Jane's pain and despair – and my inability to take it away.

When Jane and I met, I was in my late twenties and hadn't started running. If I succeed, I'll be fifty by the time I put on a Team GB vest. Is that plausible? Is it possible to be an international athlete in your fifties? I'll soon find out, but I know it's been done before. Perhaps you have to want it a little bit more and you have to train a bit smarter as you get older. After all, in our later years, we're in our prime for any test of determination, self-awareness and mental strength.

It's been a long path here. As I watch the kettle boil, I may be tired and sore, but I'm excited by the challenge that lies ahead. Over the next hour, my body will wake up. During the next three weeks, as the training load decreases, the fatigue will gradually fade away. My legs will be fresher with each day and in the final week I should be able to rest my mind and prepare myself for what lies ahead.

I know that time is not on my side, but that knowledge can be a great gift; when you can't be sure you'll have another chance, you make the best of the one you have.

PART ONE

12:00 TO 15:59

11:59 STARTING OUT

This dash to the starting line is not quite what I had planned! With twenty-four hours of running ahead of me, each step feels as though it's using a precious resource I'd prefer to have saved for the race. The morning has flown by. We arrived under heavy grey cloud almost three hours ago, to ensure we'd find a place on the grass verge beside the track where we could park the cars and pitch the gazebo and tents. We squeezed in between the outside lane and the perimeter fence, one camp in a line of many, there to shelter the support crews from the predicted downpour. Despite the city, there is a peaceful, almost rural feel to the setting, with the track surrounded by the trees of Tooting Common.

I nervously passed the time. Staying warm, going to the bathroom, reading my notes, pinning and re-pinning my race numbers on my shorts and shirt until they were perfectly centred, and generally doing my best to stay calm and positive. Then all at once, the hours and minutes had slipped by.

A sudden rush. Norman runs beside me, imparting some last-minute advice that I only half absorb. Soon I've taken my place with the other forty-six runners, light rain falling on our jumble of caps, woollen hats and bare heads.

We are a motley crew. I've read about many of these athletes before, in blogs and race reports. Some of the faces are familiar; several are famous in the rapidly expanding world of ultrarunning, others are legends in the smaller community of 24-hour events. We're all listed in the official race programme, and I try to match some of the faces I don't recognise with their names and achievements.

There are a few hellos, a soft hum of conversation and some nervous laughter. We stand and shiver, united in our nervous energy.

With seconds to go before the starting gun sounds, I remind myself to start slowly, and that I'm here because today there's no place in the world I would rather be. Then I say a quick prayer: 'Please let everyone get home safely.' It feels too much to ask for more than this. I look down the track, swallow hard and remind myself that when this is over, whatever happens, Jane will still love me – and because of that, I need fear nothing.

And then we are off.

12:00 BEGIN AT THE BEGINNING
0.00 MILES

The great ultrarunner Lizzy Hawker has spoken about standing at the starting line of the 100-mile Ultra-Trail du Mont-Blanc and recalling a quote from *Alice in Wonderland*. I carry a tweaked version of it in my mind: 'Begin at the beginning, go on until you come to the end and then stop.'

In the months leading up to the race, I've experienced moments of fear, when the idea of running for twenty-four hours seemed absurd, a huge leap into unknown territory. Those instances felt like brief moments of clarity. I would need to run more than 150 miles in one day – surely an impossible distance. However, with anything so vast, it is important to keep things simple. The first step is just to start. *Begin at the beginning.*

We are already well separated and there are three or four runners ahead of me. There are plenty of cheers from our supporters as we make our way around the first bend and back towards the starting line. I smile and wave, enjoying the moment and aware that the novelty will not last long, for us or our supporters.

It's a relief to finally be racing, after all the months of planning and imagining. The adrenaline makes movement almost effortless, and my legs feel rested and strong. I step onto the timing mat and check the split on my watch: one minute and fifty-seven seconds. I know I need to run around the track over 600 times, in which context this one lap might seem almost meaningless. Except that it is everything: it's the start, and the only path that can lead to the second lap.

Begin at the beginning. It has begun.

12:06 EVE
0.74 MILES

Even during these moments of intense focus, it is impossible not to feel some sadness. It is at the edges of my every thought, and I see it in Jane's face as I run past her. It finds a way into everything. Her mother's illness has consumed our past two months. Jane, the kindest and most loyal of daughters, has devoted herself to her mother's wellbeing, and the imminent loss in her life looms so large that everything else is overshadowed by it.

Eve is 7 miles away. I know that she would give anything to be here, next to Jane, handing me a drink and cheering me on. She's stood by the side of the road numerous times, looking for me during the London Marathon, or watching me run in Victoria Park. She has listened to my plans without once casting doubt on them. Her father, Robert Banks, was a top middle-distance runner, one good enough to run in the highly prestigious Emsley Carr Mile. Eve has told me many times that he would have loved that I run. I know she's thinking about me and will be urging me on, waiting to hear the result and hoping to celebrate my qualification for Great Britain.

This run has been a year and a half in the planning, but the final decision to race was only taken yesterday. The nurses do not expect Eve to leave us today, but no one can know for sure. After all, twenty-four hours is a long time for someone as ill as her. Jane's sister Anni will take care of Eve throughout the race and will let Jane know if anything changes and she needs to get to the hospice.

I could look up at any time and see that Jane is leaving.

What would I do? Or even worse, what would I do if I were to find out after twenty-three hours that Eve has died? We've discussed this possibility, as unreal and morbid as that may seem. We know that Eve wants me to make the qualification standard. She would not want me to leave the race if I were a few miles short of the required distance. After all, the body and mind can only deliver a performance in this kind of event, at the level I need, perhaps once a year.

Even if Eve would want me to carry on, what about Jane? My place would be with her. I'd have to leave, immediately, no matter what.

The past two months have been an emotional drain. Everything, including this race, has been to some degree deprived of its usual depth of meaning. I'm worried, for even the smallest erosion in my motivation could lead to my falling short of the mental strength I'll need. When I'm sore, tired and feeling ill, carrying on has to be the most important thing in the world. And how could I bear to see Eve in her final days or hours and say, *I'm sorry, I didn't do it. Let's see what happens next time.*

12:16 STAYING IN THE PRESENT
1.98 MILES

Fifteen minutes done. I smile, thinking back to the first of my longer training runs on the track. For me, long runs are normally all about 'park hunting' – running through as many of London's parks as possible – or else I head out on one of the canals or the Thames Path. But the best way to find out what running around a track for hours on end will be like is to do it, so I planned a four-hour session.

This training run took place early on a Saturday morning at Hampstead Heath in North London, and I had the track to myself. I started running and looked at my watch after each lap. I was interested in the time each one had taken (the 'split') in order to gauge my pace, but I also found it impossible not to look at the total time that had elapsed. After a lot of settling in, hugging the inside line around the bends and trying to relax and enjoy myself, I'd run for just fifteen minutes. Four hours was going to feel interminable!

I carried on, already looking forward to the drink I was going to have after thirty minutes. The bottles lay waiting for me next to the track, so I could simulate drinking during the race. Around me, the park was starting to come to life. Dog walkers had been joined by families out for a morning excursion. Children went past on bicycles, and a fitness group gathered under the glare of a trainer dressed in military fatigues. A few crows clustered together on the grass in the middle of the track, then flew into the air. A clutch of teenage athletes arrived in ones and twos and started to warm up, chatting and jogging on the outside lanes as they waited for their coach to arrive. Soon they started their training, running two laps at a time. I listened carefully for them to approach so I could get out of the inside lane, their youthful energy a wonder to behold each time they passed.

Before I knew it, it was time for my first drink. Then I was on my second, and then my third. I kept on looking at my watch to see the split for each lap, but now each one disappeared into an increasingly meaningless cloud of time. I was late to take my next drink, because I hadn't registered the approach of that half-hour.

Then I was alone again and in relative peace. A young man scrambled over the fence, sprinted frantically once around the track and left by the same route. The crows returned. I began to recognise the pattern of wear on the track, the battle between moss and grass at the edges of the field. And then four hours passed and it was done.

Today, the first fifteen minutes have not flown by, but that's okay. I can feel the time start to soften. At first it is difficult to not count the laps, but soon they are just a thing that happens, like the ticking of a clock.

I watch carefully, mapping my path through the runners ahead. In most ultramarathons, the field spreads out quickly and you can run for hours without seeing another competitor; here, we will be together throughout. Each runner could be passed hundreds of times. Jackets become familiar, as do the shape of legs and hats and the backs of heads.

Every lap is filled with decisions: pass inside, pass outside, dodge a puddle or run straight through it. My legs feel okay and I begin to relax; my ankle is fine. The pace is good and not too fast. I decide for now to stick with the short-sleeve shirt I'm wearing.

A leaf falls on the track, and then another.

12:30 EATING
3.72 MILES

As I approach the bend, I can see Jane standing in about the fourth lane. I've reached my first milestone. Every half an hour, I'll grab a bit of food from my crew, run the rest of the bend and then briskly walk the 100 metres to the end of the straight while eating. This will give me regular top-ups of energy and the break should make it easier for me to get the food down. Then, when I come past on the next lap, I'll be handed a drink – either water or water containing a lemon-flavoured hydration tablet – and I'll drink that as I run, handing the bottle back when I next come past.

The thirty-minute intervals between feeds will create regular milestones, helping to keep my head fixed on a limited horizon. To think about how much is still to come will not be helpful, so if my mind drifts off ahead, it will hopefully go no further than the next walk break.

With my first milestone in the bag, I have a mental image of picking something up and placing it behind me. It is the feeling of collecting laps, of building and creating. I make an effort to smile as I take the food from Jane: half an energy bar. The plan is to eat solid food early on in the race, before my system starts to shut down. I also hope that savoury foods will be less likely to make me sick than sugary ones; perhaps I'll be able to stomach some sports gels and drinks later on in the race, when solid food is impossible to swallow.

The bar goes down okay, although I find it difficult to chew as it's become harder in the cold and the oats cling to my teeth. I haven't finished it by the end of the straight, so have to continue eating as I run around the next bend. This isn't part of the plan, but it reminds me that the plan is simply an informed wish list imposed on an unpredictable reality.

12:42 GETTING OLDER
5.21 MILES

I've been looking forward to running on the same track as Geoff Oliver. I recognise him from the photographs; there have been a few articles about him in the media, and he's the subject of reverential whispers in the ultrarunning community. His persistent shuffle is easy to spot, even though he's now wrapped in long trousers and a waterproof jacket. And of all the runners competing in the race, he's the only one who is eighty-five years old.

Just five years ago, on this same track, Geoff ran 100 miles in twenty-four hours, which surely must be one of the greatest athletic achievements of all time. To be on the track with him is a huge privilege, and I'll be watching his progress and willing him on.

I was in a café some years ago when the waiter told me that at forty-one, he was too old to start running. I explained that many of my friends had been older than that when they started running and had made it part of their lives. It was clear he was unable to challenge his preconceptions – as far as he was concerned, he was already washed up.

Nowhere in running is age less of an issue than in ultrarunning. After all, losing a yard of speed over a mile matters a lot less when the race is 100 miles long. At the end of events like the 24-Hour World Championships, the athletes on the podium might be in their twenties, but they will more likely be in their thirties, forties or even their fifties.

One of the greatest runners in history, Yiannis Kouros, once told *Runner's World* magazine: 'The older you are, the better for ultrarunning, because mental experience is much more important than physical speed.' The best ultrarunners are still reasonably quick over shorter distances, because speed will always transfer to any distance. What is more important is that they will be mentally strong and possess the maturity not to run too fast at the start. They will have the life skills necessary to prepare and cope. Some people gain these traits at an early age; Great Britain's Robbie Britton, who won bronze at the 24-Hour European Championships in his mid-twenties, is a good example.

Geoff Oliver won't win today's race. Nor will the incredible Patricia Seabrook, seventy-eight years old and a prolific marathon and ultrarunner who will be hoping to complete as many miles in this race as she has spent years on the planet. And nor will Ann Bath, who two years ago ran over 115 miles in twenty-four hours, at the age of sixty-eight.

The years do have an effect, but these athletes show us what is possible if we apply ourselves, have a fair bit of luck, and continue to believe in our ability. As elite athletes, it's true they are among the best in the world for their age groups, but if Geoff Oliver can run around the track for twenty-four hours at the age of eighty-five, then maybe someone who thought they were too old can decide to go for a jog for the first time, or maybe that forty-one-year-old waiter can rethink what he might be able to achieve. As for me, I'll watch my fellow participants run through these hours and will never forget what I see.

12:51 BEING WATCHED
6.46 MILES

On the side of the track stands a photographer. The race website has lots of photos from last year's race and I'm guessing he's the source of them. I spent a lot of time looking at those photos, trying to work out how often I'd need to leave the inside lane to overtake other runners – just how full is a track with forty-five athletes? It turns out that I'd wasted my time worrying; yes, I'm having to run further than I would like on most laps, but there was never going to be anything I could do about it. Everyone is considerate but it's impossible to always move out of the way for faster runners. There are a few lapping me and I don't always hear them in time to get out of their way.

During my mental preparation, those photos did also help me visualise what the race would be like, so perhaps the time was not poorly spent. However, something I didn't anticipate was the long lens of the camera pointing at *me*. There's a gap of about 30 metres between me and the lens, with no other runner in the way, and I start to feel a little self-conscious. Should I smile? Give a thumbs-up? Those are the kinds of photos that often appear on race websites: the big grins, the waves, the runners leaping into the air. Less often does the anxious grimace or the bent form of the vomiting athlete appear. I suppose I could smile, but instead I run stiffly past, trying hard to act natural.

When you're young, everyone is looking at you, assessing, judging and talking about you. Then at some point you realise that they are spending at least some of their time thinking everyone is watching and talking about *them*. When you grow up some more, you realise that people have other things on their minds. For me, this was a process of both evolution and moments of epiphany. While it's disappointing to discover that you are not the centre of the universe, the upside is that you have less reason to feel self-conscious.

Still, sometimes we work hard to project a certain image. My working life was made a lot easier by one otherwise minor incident. I was a media spokesperson for our company and my colleague Jacques Sellschop, who ran the public relations department, arranged for a photographer to take some photos of me. The next day, he spread some prints out on his desk so we could choose which one to use.

'That one,' I said. I looked serious, strong and older, not to be trifled with.

'Interesting,' he said. 'I was thinking about this one.' He pointed to a photo in which I was smiling. I was young at the time, but I looked even younger in the picture. What on earth was he thinking?

With the certainty of experience and good intentions, he continued. 'That's perhaps how you see yourself,' he said, pointing to the one I had chosen, 'but *this* is how *we* see you.' I had put a lot of effort into coming across as serious, hard and older – and it turned out I was fooling no one.

It was a revelation. Over the following days, I started to feel much more relaxed. Sitting in meetings, I didn't bother trying to convey anything other than competence. I was more confident in being me, and my working life became less exhausting as a result.

I suppose there will still always be times when we feel self-conscious, but in London it's easy to do whatever you want and know that no one cares. Before a race where the weather could be hot, I do heat-acclimatisation training. Within a couple of weeks, your body and mind are able to make adjustments that make running in the heat a bit easier. If it's not hot enough outside, I wear extra clothes while training, and sometimes I run on the treadmill in the gym, where it's warmer and there's no breeze to cool me down. I then add layers of clothes to make myself hotter. The first time I got on the treadmill at my gym wearing running tights, a heavy rain jacket, a beanie, a scarf and mittens, I felt quite self-conscious. I waited for the stares and the comments, but no one said a word.

I'm soon approaching the photographer again. I don't smile, wave or jump in the air, but nor do I try to look athletic, or run faster. And this time I don't *try* to act natural. I don't know what I do – I just do it.

13:10 TIME, DISTANCE AND PLACING
8.69 MILES

Just inside the track, at the starting line, is the race organisers' gazebo, which houses two major attractions. The first is the race clock, which sits on a folding table, displaying the hours, minutes and seconds in bright yellow digits. 'Don't look at the clock' is a common piece of advice given to first-time runners. It is thought that clock-watching causes the time to drag. This is all very well in theory, but ignoring a clock that is over a metre long is much harder in reality!

Next to the clock and over two metres tall is the second major attraction: the leaderboard. It will be updated every hour to show the distance each participant has run, our names moved up or down as our positions change.

For the past ten minutes, I've been waiting for the distances to go up. I know it's too early to worry about placings, but I'm already keen to see how things stand. After a flurry of activity around the board, names and numbers start to appear. I'm in fourth place, with seven miles. Of course, I might have reached seven miles a second before the one-hour mark or I might have been one yard short of eight. I must remember later not to be dispirited if my distance doesn't leap up as quickly as I feel it should; I might always have been just short of the next mile.

The board will be my companion through the night, guiding and informing me about my progress. I try not to think about tomorrow and what the board will say at the end. All that matters is now, and the twenty minutes between me and my next feed.

13:55 SOMEWHERE IN SOUTH LONDON
14.41 MILES

Outside these tree-lined boundaries of the running track, the world carries on. Cars crawl past, planes fly overhead and people go about their normal lives. It is us here, life in microcosm, and them there, on the other side of the fence.

Perhaps in the park next door a family is out for a walk, oblivious to what we are doing. Come quickly – there's an eighty-five-year-old man running for twenty-four hours just on the other side of those trees! Come and see for yourself and show your children so that they don't ever forget what's possible.

How can it be that people can just pass by, unaware? I imagine a satellite image of the race on a computer screen. There's a grassy field enclosed by a synthetic track. People are running around it, observed by others from a ring of grass and cement, with trees all around them.

I zoom out, and the area displayed by the map grows to include a park, houses and major roads. In a park somewhere in South London, a child walks for the first time. A wife prepares to leave her husband. Two people find each other, after years alone.

I zoom out again and the world is bigger still. Amazing human stories are separated by a fence or a road. How many do I walk past every day? What microcosms of human existence do I pass on a single training run?

Somewhere in South London, a seventy-eight-year-old woman is running around a track for twenty-four hours – and no one says a word.

14:06 TOUGHNESS
15.65 MILES

If there's a song that has got me thinking about this race over the past few months, it is 'Tougher Than the Rest' by Bruce Springsteen. I didn't set out to find a song with a corny motivational mantra in its lyrics, but it seemed to be in my head at key times during my training. The toughness Springsteen is talking about is the ability to handle love, but I guess he knows toughness comes in many forms.

The people on this running track are all undoubtedly blessed with toughness. In order just to be here, they have put themselves through the wringer, physically and mentally. Most of them have run through at least one night. They have run in the heat and the freezing cold, through rain and snow and through everything that the elements and their own bodies and minds have thrown at them in a vain attempt to make them stop.

Mari Mauland, the Norwegian ultrarunner, is one of the favourites for the women's race and also stands a chance of winning the event outright. There's a wonderful line from her report of the Bislett 24-Hour Indoor Challenge that I like to quote – for me, it perfectly captures the shifting sense of normality that comes from the repeated exposure to difficult circumstances that ultrarunners encounter. She said, 'Vomiting aside, the 10km from 150km to 100 miles went pretty smoothly, so I decided to continue until I'd reached 200km.'

The British international Sarah Morwood is another potential winner. It takes me a while to spot her – I've seen plenty of photographs of her, but identifying someone from behind when they're wearing a rain hood is a different proposition. After she fractured her knee in a collision with a car while cycling, Sarah was told she might never run again, but she came through the long period of rehabilitation and fought back to represent Great Britain in the Trail World Championships.

Tom Garrod was in his twenties when he was diagnosed with stage 4 testicular cancer. He was expected to die, but a year later he had successfully come through treatment and held the record for running the length of Ireland. Now he combines his competitive ultrarunning with his campaign to raise awareness of the illness.

Sinead Kane is blind and has three guide runners who will take turns to run alongside her during the race. The female world record holder for 12 hours on a treadmill, she is a runner of serious quality. I have no real insight to the specific challenges of running while blind, but the risk of accident and injury must be significantly higher. Merely gauging the curve of the bends in the track hundreds of times, as exhaustion sets in, must surely be a unique exercise of concentration.

Everyone out here has a story to tell – of injuries, mental and physical illness, personal sacrifice, survival, extremes of emotion and many miles of relentless training and racing. Anyone here could be 'tougher than the rest', but it would be a brave person to make that claim in such incredible company.

14:12 FOCUS
16.40 MILES

When the race programme was published, I quickly scanned through the list of entrants. Later that day, I was on the phone with Norm and started talking about some of the runners who might be trying to obtain the standard for GB selection. Instead of the discussion about my tactics for the race I was expecting, it was a very short conversation.

'Just focus on your own performance,' he said. 'It doesn't matter what the other runners do.'

Now I'm about to lap Marco Consani. I met his wife – Debbie Martin-Consani, also a GB international – before the race, but not him. When I introduce myself, it feels momentous. I've read a lot about him and to meet him on the track is special. He's friendly and encouraging, and tells me I'm doing well.

'I'm a bit worried to be in front of you,' I say. Marco is a top-flight runner with a great deal of experience and an astute understanding of pacing. Should I be going faster than him so early in the race? He laughs and tells me I'm doing just fine.

I think about it some more and really feel I'm running at the right pace. Focusing on my own performance means not running faster in order to keep up with someone else, but it also means not slowing down for fear of passing them. Marco has a great record, but that will count for little if he isn't yet fully fit after injury problems that he's suffered from earlier in the year. Or he may just prefer to start more slowly than would suit me. If I focus on his performance instead of my own, I could lose my way.

We wish each other well and I ease ahead. He may pass me later, but I'm confident that this is how I should be running to get the best possible result at noon tomorrow.

Am I actually racing against anybody at all? I have finite resources that I need to make last until the finish. If I do it well, I will have run as far as is possible for me, and if someone can go further than my best distance, there was never anything I could have done about it anyway.

In my mind, I can see a line graph plotting the distance of each of us on the track over the twenty-four hours. My line is based on the optimum use of my energy resources – I like its shape. There are other lines, each with their own shape, and where they finish is beyond my control.

I'll focus on my own performance. Maybe in the final hour I'll find myself in a race with someone else, but until then it's just me and my line.

14:17 A FEMALE WINNER?
16.90 MILES

Whoever runs the furthest in this race will be awarded with two trophies: one for first male or female, and another for overall winner. There is a real possibility that the overall winner will be a woman. It has happened in this race before, and it is fairly common in ultras.

At the 2011 Commonwealth Mountain and Ultradistance Running Championships, Lizzy Hawker set a new women's world record for the 24-hour event, beating all the male athletes in the process. Debbie Martin-Consani won the prestigious 145-mile Grand Union Canal Race some years ago, and American greats Courtney Dauwalter and Camille Herron both often win events outright, with very few men in the world capable of beating them. Sometimes the woman who wins will be the fastest over shorter distances too, but often it is not the fastest runner who wins anyway. In ultrarunning, speed and power only count for so much; endurance, racing intelligence and mental strength are just as important. And the longer the race, the greater the advantages of having a strong mind.

The thing that surprises me the most is how surprised we are when women win. Yet often a female athlete is the standout world-class runner in the field. Do women have any specific advantages when it comes to long races, like mental fortitude or superior fat-burning abilities? Whatever the reason, I've been passed by enough elite women in the final quarter of the 56-mile Comrades Marathon to believe that, on average, women pace their races better than men, a skill that over longer races can be even more beneficial.

As more women take up ultrarunning, there will be more female outright winners – perhaps we'll eventually learn not to be surprised.

14:28 AN EVOLVING SENSE OF POSSIBILITY
18.39 MILES

For the runner who has just completed their first 5km race and is thinking about attempting 10km, the idea of running twice as far may be a daunting prospect. A few months later though, it may well be that they have run 10km and the 5km distance no longer holds any fear. The half marathon, more than twice as far, may seem a long way off, but is not as unattainable as it once seemed. The marathon is still a remote possibility – that is, until they're at the finish line of their first half marathon.

Deciding to take the leap, they may begin marathon training. Their long weekend run gradually creeps up in distance, until one day they are looking at themselves in the mirror, amazed that they have run for 20 miles. 'How will I ever do those final six though?' they ask, given how tired and sore they feel after 20. But whether they know it or not, they have probably already done enough to convince their brain that 26.2 miles is possible.

My first ultra-distance race was the 56-mile Comrades Marathon in South Africa. The distance is effectively two marathons plus a 5km, and is run over hilly terrain. It was a significant increase in distance and a real step up from the marathon. The prospect was daunting, but a few things were in my favour.

Like many other ultrarunners, I had doubled the distances I raced: 10km to a half marathon, half marathon to a marathon. So, to do so again did not seem beyond the bounds of logic and reason.

Then, just as marathon runners do 20-mile training runs, I had done some training runs that, while well short of the race distance, were still further than halfway. I convinced my mind that 56 miles was possible.

The length of the marathon is an arbitrary distance created by an accident of history and made famous by our human desire to challenge ourselves. The distance of 26.2 miles isn't the point at which human capability ends, any more than 10km or 38.65432 miles is; it is simply a distance that has captured our collective imagination. A lot of runners who run marathons every year have never run a yard further. There is, of course, no reason why they should, unless they are keen to explore ultrarunning and are hesitant simply because they regard the marathon as some mythical upper limit. This limitation, they should realise, is simply a mindset.

My first run that was longer than a marathon was a 34-mile training run. When I didn't explode or hit any metaphorical walls, my assumptions changed completely and I gained a whole new sense of possibility – not only as a runner, but also as a person. I left my house one morning, ran on my own and returned some hours later. I took off my shoes, had something to eat, showered and collapsed on the sofa, with an immense sense of achievement. *I could run further than a marathon.* But more than that, in terms of my own identity, I could do so without fanfare or kudos – it felt empowering to do something simply because I wanted to do it. And it was also powerful to know that I could do it again, whenever I wanted to.

I felt the same way some years later, after my first 50-mile training run. There is something surreal about returning home having run 50 miles as if it were just another day. A couple of hours later, I set out to buy a bar of chocolate from the corner shop and a neighbour told me I looked tired and asked if I was unwell. 'No, I'm fine thanks,' I replied. 'I've just been out running so am a bit worn out.'

I was lucky to grow up watching normal people from all walks of life run 56 miles in the Comrades Marathon on TV, just as kids might watch the great city marathons now. My father completed the Comrades three times, and I was there to watch him twice. His glorious entrance to the stadium at the end of the race and the sight of the iconic medal around his neck were powerful images for a child.

I love watching children running in a Park Run with their parents, or when they are there to watch their parents complete a race, be it a 10km, a marathon or something longer. It creates a personal association with possibility – if someone they know can run a 10km, why shouldn't they? This sense of possibility is invaluable, whether they decide to run themselves in their teens, their twenties, or, like me, many years later.

For those who don't have this gift from childhood, having the courage to take the first step is a great achievement. I always knew that running was an option for me and had enough knowledge of training to make starting in my thirties fairly easy, but some people have to overcome a complete lack of knowledge and various negative preconceptions before they can begin. One of the great achievements of Park Runs has been making getting started much more accessible.

Someone who decides to run 100 yards for the first time has created a new sense of possibility: they are now someone who runs. For many people, this opens an entirely new association with their physical self. When they look in the mirror, they see a runner looking back at them.

Months, years or decades later, their focus could be anything from collecting Park Runs, targeting personal bests and running long distances to simply running with friends. They may never wake up with the hunger to run for twenty-four hours, but one day, if their interest evolves in that direction, it may start to seem completely plausible to do so. And more than plausible: maybe even a good idea.

14:45 A LABOUR OF LOVE
20.38 MILES

Shankara Smith is sweeping the track. The rain is collecting in puddles across the first and second lanes, and she's taking every opportunity between passing athletes to clear the water away with a broom. It helps, and I tell her this as I go by. It means less of the endless decision-making; whether to avoid the puddle, jump over it, step towards the shallow end or just plunge right through. None of these options are great for my efficiency and rhythm, and to see even one of the puddles getting slightly smaller gives me a mental boost.

Shankara plays a big role in this event. She and her fellow Race Director, Devashishu Torpy, contribute more than just organisational excellence – there's a positive energy here that comes from genuine passion and commitment. This is not just a race, it is a piece of history, and the vision of the event's founder, Ongkar Tony Smith, realised year after year. People care deeply about it.

Shankara works her way around the track, smiling as the raindrops hit her hat. To the right is the makeshift kitchen where our crews will be fed throughout the night. I recall a video from a previous year of a young woman managing the kitchen, who radiated such happiness at playing her part in the event. I hope she's there again today, looking after Jane and my crew.

Now I pass the start and the line of human lap counters who will sit for hours in the cold, concentrating on our progress yet still managing to smile and wave each time we pass. There is electronic timing to count our laps automatically, but the human counters are a back-up, as well as a tradition that contributes hugely to the DNA of the event.

Shankara won't beat the puddles – it will soon be raining harder and her team will need her elsewhere. However, the fact that she tries is one of the many things that makes this event what it is: a labour of love.

15:09 A FEW SPECIAL HOURS REQUIRE MANY ORDINARY DAYS
23.36 MILES

There came a time in my life when the days and weeks at first seemed to drift but then started to slip by more quickly. I realised that life is finite and as I reached the end of a week, I would wonder what I had achieved. Had I experienced joy? Did I live for every moment? Was I fully engaged with life?

Last night, as I prepared for the race, I flicked through my logbook, in which I keep a record of every training run. It's good to remind myself of the work I've done to prepare for a race. As I read the distances and notes, I also remembered a few of those runs: an evening when everything just clicked and I felt invincible, a time when I looked out over London from Alexandra Palace in the glorious sunshine, a moment when I felt suddenly like an athlete as I flew down a hill, a run in the fresh snow and a long run on the treadmill when the snow had turned to ice. The rest of the runs were just names and numbers, their individuality lost in the anonymity of my training regime. '10 miles easy, feeling okay.'

And now, a day that will live with me forever. *What else could I be doing today to engage more fully with life?* I'm taking myself to unknown emotional, mental and physical extremes, striving for a level of sporting achievement that once seemed utterly impossible for me. I'm seeking to open new doors by deploying everything I have in one massive effort at achieving personal greatness: the most that I can become with the gifts and limitations that are unique to me.

I spent the five days before the race doing as little as possible

– resting up and switching off the body and mind to anything that felt like effort. It was like I was hibernating. Over these past months, I have lost many things to tiredness and the need to rest: opportunities to make new friends, to see art exhibitions, to climb a mountain. But it was all for this.

If I do my best today, I will not look back and feel regret for all the paths not followed. At most, I will feel a gentle pathos and an understanding that many ordinary days are required to make a few great ones.

15:30 GOALS
26.1 MILES

I must be somewhere around the marathon mark now. I don't expect it to be noted by the counters or my crew, but I always like to take note of milestones – they add to the sense of building and collecting as the race progresses.

I remember finishing an 8-mile run many years ago. It was the furthest I had ever run and one of the first times I thought seriously about doing a marathon. But the difference between what I had just done and 26.2 miles was almost unfathomable – it would mean running more than three times as far! Then, bit by bit, my context evolved until the marathon was run and the distance was no longer the challenge – it became all about the time. At first the dream was to run in under three hours. When I achieved that at the Rotterdam Marathon, Jane hugged me and said, 'You did it, you're free!' We laugh about that now, because it was the beginning rather than the end, and the only freedom it gave me was to create more ambitious targets: faster marathons and longer races.

Today I have plenty of targets, but I'm not confusing them with my goal, which is to be running in the final minutes. If I'm still running after twenty-four hours, then all the things I want to achieve will flow from that: a GB-qualifying distance and a place on the podium. But if I chase those things, I'm much more likely to make a mistake – like going out too fast.

The performance is everything; I just have to do the right things at the right time, and the rest will take care of itself. The need to be capable of running at the end determines how fast I run now. The outcomes I want from the race will take centre stage in the final hours, but not before then.

My other goal is to do my best, whatever the circumstances. If things unravel for any reason and I cannot run all the way, then the goal is to run as far as I can in the time I have and to see where it takes me.

My brain knows what I am capable of in terms of speed and endurance because it was there when I raced and trained. It has listened to everything I have said, to myself and others, and it has heard what has been said to me. It can work out how fast I should be going at any point. My main job is to manage the wildcards that might get in the way of what my brain knows is possible: ego, bravado, false assumptions, the sense of occasion, overambition and all the things the other parts of my brain will throw at me in an attempt to change my mind.

I've come a long way from that first 8-mile run. Like many runners, that path is paved with many goals that have been realised not by the pursuit of people or splits on a watch, but by focusing on getting the most from myself on that day.

PART TWO

16:00 TO 19:59

16:00 CHANGING DIRECTION
29.82 MILES

The biggest landmarks in this race will be the changes of direction that take place every four hours. Despite having looked forward to it for the last half-hour, it comes as a shock to see an athlete running towards me in the second lane. She must have already rounded the traffic cone placed just beyond the timing mat at the starting line.

Soon there are other runners heading my way in the second or third lane. Some of them are smiling while others are serious, and a few of them seem to be struggling. I offer a couple of high-fives as I head towards the cone myself, and then I'm turning around and running back towards those who are yet to make the change. I can't help but let out a joyful exclamation at having passed such a major milestone. I've often imagined how this change will feel, and here I am at last.

It feels strange to see the faces as they come past and to connect each one to a jacket, hat or hood that I've glanced at so many times during the past four hours. Some are a surprise: while running in the same direction, in most cases I've glimpsed only a profile, and I must have added features to them in my imagination. In many cases, we wish each other well. Our celebration is heartfelt but cautious; after all, we will do this four more times before we can progress into the final four-hour block.

As I get to the first bend, the change is a little disconcerting – all my previous turns have been to the right and now I'm suddenly turning to the left. The sights are also different; what was previously familiar is now a new landscape of angles, shapes and images – it feels like I'm in another dimension that badly mimics our own. Still, as I pass Jane and take my drink from her, I'm smiling at the novelty of it all.

16:05 THE FEELING
30.32 MILES

Is running addictive? If I'm addicted to anything it is *the feeling*, but it is so short-lived and so unreliable that it never seems certain. *The feeling* is not reason enough to lace up my shoes and I don't even think of it when I set off on a long run, but when it comes, it reminds me of why I love to run.

When I get *the feeling*, there is no endorphin rush or soaring mood. Instead there is tiredness, discomfort and grounded reflection. To get to *the feeling* takes plenty of effort: for me it normally comes in the 5 miles after the marathon distance, if at all. For others it might come at another time, especially if their focus is on shorter distances. I have had *the feeling* a couple of times on a hard hike or long bike ride, and it is always a product of significant effort.

The feeling is a composite of physical and mental sensations. It is a tiredness that suddenly becomes pleasant, as the legs move well despite the pain. It is a realisation that the body is doing something it is designed to do and the recognition that it is doing something out of the ordinary.

The feeling cannot be bought or guaranteed; it simply happens. Perhaps there's a physiological element, such as a point at which fat use is optimised, but I like to think of it as a magical moment when the body and mind are perfectly in tune with each other. Both have accepted what is happening and what still needs to be done, and both have pushed the buttons that will result in the best possible performance. And, for a short while, before the arguments start, they are one.

16:13 BEING LIGHT
31.31 MILES

Being light is good. When you're light, it is easier to propel yourself around the track. Being light improves the body's power-to-weight ratio. Being light feels athletic and mentally advantageous. Being light is the promise of success and the confirmation of fitness. Being light is evident in the lines of the ribs, the twists of sinew in the shoulders and the muscles rippling across the stomach. It is the tightest notch in a belt.

Light is a number on a scale. Light is one treat away from unfit, one bite away from heavy. It is a state of mind and a mood that comes and goes. Light is an ephemeral promise, the seduction of control. Light is remorse, obsession and self-loathing. Light is good, until it isn't.

Does being lighter equate to running further and faster? I feel the strength now; the power of a machine designed and maintained for economy and endurance. There's not much fat on the machine, though my stomach is not quite the rippling perfection of my athletic dreams.

At a certain weight, I start to feel feeble. I've been fortunate to recoil instinctively from that feeling and quickly put on weight, but the thought persists: *will being lighter make me better?*

Before my first call with nutritionist Renee McGregor, I researched the body mass index of elite runners; from what I could tell, I was at the heavy end of the scale. Would Renee, who works with many Olympic and international athletes, tell me to cut the chocolate and the calories in order to reach the next level of performance? Thankfully, she did not, which is not surprising given that she dedicates a lot of her time to highlighting the dangers of eating disorders and Relative Energy Deficiency in sport. RED is the insufficient nutritional intake to meet the demands of training, which can have catastrophic consequences for body and mind. Being lighter, she said, would more likely deliver mental or physical injury than progress.

Like most athletes, I am very aware of my weight. I may go weeks without stepping on a set of scales, and I'm no saint when it comes to wine and treats, but there's not a day in which I don't take a decision to decline or moderate. Keeping to a healthy weight is one of the benefits of running, but an engagement with when and what to eat can easily morph into an unhealthy obsession or a destructive quest for unachievable goals. The lure for any runner is obvious: *I reckon I could cut a couple of minutes off my personal best for every kilogram I shed. Imagine two kilos. Or four. Or, eight!* This is fine if the runner is carrying a lot of excess weight, but not if they are already trim. Running is also a hiding place for eating disorders, because the extremely thin runner will have plenty of company and can gain approval and adulation for their thinness from those who are unaware of their problem.

Renee was happy with me as I was. My fear of fragility keeps me on the right side of the line, though it's easy to take a misstep in a moment of weakness and find yourself on the wrong side of it. Or to obsess too much and stare so hard at the line that you lose the ability to see it at all.

Being light is only good if it is a natural state, the meeting point of hard training and healthy eating. A feeling of fitness and strength accompanied by a positive sense of self. Being light for the sake of it spells danger.

16:57 GENEROSITY OF SPIRIT
36.78 MILES

'Come on, Michael.' The voice belongs to James Elson, a member of the Great Britain 24-hour running team and the Race Director for Centurion Running, who organise some wonderful ultramarathons in the UK. He's chatting with friends at the side of the track and offering his support.

At least four of the men running today are trying to achieve the qualification standard to run for Great Britain at the 24-Hour World Championships. There are six places available in each of the men's and women's teams, and there are already more runners who have met the standard than places. We are competing for the chance to represent our country; a chance that comes only once a year at the World or European championships.

Twelve months ago, James and I both ran the Downslink Ultra, a point-to-point race in Sussex along a disused railway that has been converted into a path. I got lost twice, and the first time was with James. We were both just there for a hard training run, so were quite relaxed despite our error, and we chatted as we found our way back to the course. Later, as we ran together in second and third place, I began to drift off ahead of him. An hour or so on, I was surprised to reach a section out of character with the rest of the course; there were a couple of muddy hills and some twists and turns that, to my relief, eventually led once more to a flatter, straighter path. I saw the lead runner ahead of me and was pleased that I'd be challenging for the lead. Inch by inch, I began to reel him in. I'm not sure exactly when I realised that the person ahead of me was once again James!

At the end of the race, we sat, covered in mud, and chatted. I had won the Thames Path 100, one of his company's 100-mile races, earlier in the year and told him that I wanted to try to achieve the British 24-hour standard at some point in the following year. He was very encouraging and began to share his experience with me, including advice on which races he thought would give me the best chance of reaching the required distance.

During the following week, I received an email from John Pares, Chief Selector and Team Manager for Great Britain's 24-hour squad. James had told him that I was targeting the 24-hour standard and he'd got in touch to talk to me about the set-up and to offer encouragement. I then had an inspiring call with him and Robbie Britton. John and Robbie both seemed to think I was a serious contender to run the GB standard, which was a huge boost for my self-belief, and I had James to thank for putting me on their radar.

James has also encouraged another runner, Paul Maskell, to enter today's race for his attempt at reaching the GB standard, because of the small number of other runners there will be to navigate on the track. Paul is just a mile or two behind me and has a real chance not only of achieving that standard but of winning the race as well.

In two months, James will be heading for a track in the Arizona desert to make his own attempt at a GB qualifying distance. He has made his task more difficult by selflessly helping others who are competing for places. I hope that as I watch the online video feed of his run, as he's approaching my distance I will both *say* the right thing – *Come on, James* – and also have the generosity of spirit to truly mean it.

17:03 COUNTING LAPS
37.53 MILES

Over these hours I have come to trust my lap counter. We understand each other. She wants me to do well, and she pays close attention. I have assigned to her all kinds of personality traits that likely bear no resemblance to who she is. I have also projected opinions onto her on how I'm doing in the race, about my pace and my potential result. She is counting laps for other athletes, but I am her favourite.

Change is at hand, though. As I pass, she shouts out that someone else is taking over. In the heat of the moment, I barely see his face and I don't catch his name – I'm too used to looking for her. It is a bit disconcerting; we had got into a good rhythm. I waved each time I passed, and most of the time she waved back. On the few occasions she didn't, I shouted my number. It wasn't that she wasn't paying attention – she'd be looking at the pages or screens on the table in front of her. Each of the ten or so people behind that table is counting for a number of runners, so the demands on their concentration are high. Sometimes I am alone as I approach, but on other occasions there has been a large group in which she had to spot me. I know the electronic mat is also counting each time I cross – I listen for the beep as it reads my timing chip – but the idea that I could do even one lap that goes uncounted doesn't bear thinking about.

Now the new guy is taking over and we'll have to start again, with a new face to slot into my process: look for the counter, watch for the wave of recognition, wave back, listen for the beep of the timing system, look at the lap split on my watch, realise I haven't absorbed what the watch is saying and decide that it doesn't matter. Repeat.

Now, as I approach, I don't see him.

'Got you, Michael!' The shout comes loud and clear.

He's standing behind his chair, raising his entire arm to make sure I see him. It is a relief. More than a relief, it is a revelation. Could it be that I've got lucky and have drawn the Roger Federer of counters? The next time I come around, he shouts out again. I wave. Moments later I hear a beep and look at my watch. What did it say? I've no idea, but it doesn't really matter.

What does he think about this pace, I wonder? I think he's fully on board with where we are and am sure we're going to do something special here today.

17:05 THE FEAR OF LEADING
37.78 MILES

When I look at the board as I pass, my name is at the top. I am in the lead and one mile ahead. The resulting surge of adrenaline is an unwelcome interruption to my calmness that leaves me slightly shaky and near breathless. I feel suddenly self-conscious, as if I have been running in a pack and am now on my own out in front.

A part of me is pleased. I want to win this race and being in the lead makes me feel that I can; it's a confirmation that will breed further belief. *I knew this was possible, and it's going to be just how I imagined it. It's happening.*

At the same time, I'm concerned that I'm leading at such an early point in the race. Have I started too fast? Should I really be in front of someone like the GB international Marco Consani, who is a couple of places behind me? Am I going to be completely exposed, and end up exhausted and embarrassed with many hours left to run?

The first time I was leading in a race with any prospect of winning was in a 10km race with about 500 participants. Well into the second half, it was down to four of us, then three, and then there was just me and one other guy. It was the first time I'd ever been in that situation and it was a surreal experience. We passed people waiting at the side of the road and they seemed excited to see us. This was it – the sharp end of the race – and I was one of the people there!

I'd decided years earlier that I had a good 'racing brain' and would always have the advantage of being smart. I had little to base this thought on, except some inherent self-belief and the tactical knowledge I'd absorbed from my father while watching running with him over the years. But I knew enough to know that I had to try to look past my screaming lungs and lactate-flooded limbs and think. *How can I win this? I'm not much of a sprinter, so I'll have to go early.*

As we passed the 9km mark, I put in a sudden surge and he dropped away from my shoulder. I could hear that he was still close, but he wasn't next to me – I was in the lead. It was both exhilarating and terrifying. There's a primal fear that comes from being out in front with the pursuing pack behind. The hunted, the target. And then there's the fear that's probably peculiar only to some of us: *what if I try to win and fail? Will I look stupid?*

Two hundred metres later and he was still there, just behind me. I somehow surged again, and the sound of his breathing slipped slightly further back. I sensed that he could be breaking and somehow pushed forwards again, and then I ran as if my life depended on it – it felt like it did. *This is your chance to win a race. If you do nothing else ever again, you will always have this.*

Before I knew it, I was turning into the finishing straight, with the crowd clapping as I crossed the line in agony, bliss and disbelief. I had won!

Many years later, while running my first 100-mile race along the River Thames from Richmond to Oxford, I took the lead with about 60 miles to go. If I found leading scary, I was about to get a lot of practice. I almost immediately made my only serious mistake of the race: I didn't stop for water at the next checkpoint because I wanted to put some distance between me and second place to make sure the other runner didn't feel hopeful about staying close. To do that so early on was stupid and could have cost me more than the dehydration and vomiting I eventually suffered from, but reason can be hard to come by when you're leading in a race – and that's where experience becomes invaluable.

I have more experience now. Not as much as many other runners, but enough to know to take my time and calmly think things through. My pace is right and I'm focusing on my own performance – if that happens to put me in the front, then so be it. I may be in second or third in an hour's time and that's also okay, as long as I keep doing the right things at the right time. All that matters is where things stand after twenty-four hours.

Despite this, I still feel a little bit of excitement at being in front. As I pass Jane and my crew, I wonder if they know. I imagine Jane feeling proud and the thought gives me a warm surge of happiness. I remind myself to stay calm and grounded, and not to speed up or get ahead of myself. That being in the lead in a race with nineteen hours to go is completely meaningless. But leading is a definite boost to my sense of belief. And best of all, I feel like I belong out here, at the front. It feels slightly strange, but it is not a surprise.

17:18 NEGATIVE CHATTER
39.27 MILES

'Trapped.'

I recognise that voice, the negativity. It speaks in half-formed thoughts and uses punchy, catchy phrases, like propaganda.

'No way out.'

We're fine where we are. I don't know why I answer it with 'we', but I often do.

'Tired.'

Feeling fine. I used to reason with it, but now I use the same blunt language. When I'm tired, I sometimes forget and try to present rational arguments from my hazy mind and it feels endless, the drunken philosopher arguing with the fascist.

'Not on a good day.'

Feeling good.

'Could stop for a pee.'

I don't need to pee.

'Stop for a pee, get a rest.'

Glad I don't need to rest.

'It should feel better than this.'

Feeling fine.

'Hips are already sore.'

They'll ease later.

'Immobile.'

Moving well.

How much of my energy is taken up with these arguments with myself? And after every race I forget what it was like; the near-constant negative chatter in my head. Mostly I don't answer and just try not to listen, so that the negative voice is just another signal in the static, among the random thoughts, the sound of footsteps and the reports from nerves all around my body.

In normal life the negative voice has lost much of its power over the years. Whether that is the gift of age, experience or greater self-awareness, I don't know. Its ambition withered, it largely seems focused on more humble targets. Why else do I decide it's a bad morning before I've even got out of bed? *Not a morning person.*

I said that once to Andy Barton, my mental performance coach, and he pointed out that I will certainly not be a morning person if I say I'm not. The next few mornings, I lay in bed listening to the voice as it complained like a stroppy child. I'd been so busy feeling how it wanted me to feel that I hadn't even noticed it was there. I countered each negative thought with a more helpful, positive one, and after a few days that started to work. I don't always get it right, but now I understand that taking a while to get going in the morning is a good reason to take a little bit of time sitting quietly with a coffee. And if I look forward to that part of the day, then I guess mornings are fine for me now.

A whole minute must have passed without me hearing the voice. It takes effort to bat it away, but this early in the race it is not too difficult. Later it will be louder and more and more insistent. It feeds on tiredness and seeks out weakness. It can be beaten – I have beaten it many times before – but I've never run for twenty-four hours. I hope I will be ready.

17:49 THE BEST-LAID PLANS
43.00 MILES

I'm really cold. I've been denying the fact for a while but avoiding wearing a rain jacket is not going to work any longer. The last of the feeble daylight has brought a rapid drop in temperature and the rain begins to fall more heavily. My crew have been encouraging me to wear a jacket for hours, so they are pleased when I ask for it. I also ask for a dry shirt to be prepared and immediately wonder why I didn't do this ages ago.

When I approach Jane on the next lap, she's standing on the track with the dry shirt and the jacket. The idea of being dry and warm suddenly feels like a dream. Still, keeping moving is more important than anything else and I decide to get the shirt on this lap and the jacket on the next one, to avoid stopping.

When I'm ten metres away from Jane, I slow down to a fast walk and remove the sodden shirt. I grab the replacement and throw it over my head, but it gets stuck, refusing to go past my neck. I wrestle with it for another ten yards, but it's like an elaborate puzzle. *Are my faculties so impaired that I've forgotten how to put on a shirt? Am I trying to ram my head through the armhole?* I manage to prise it off my head and discover that my race number has been attached to it with safety pins and that one of them has gone through the front and the back of the shirt, sealing it shut!

I turn back towards Jane and throw her the shirt. I still have my wet shirt in one hand and start to run while unbundling it. At this point, I'm running topless and feel like the picture of frantic disorganisation. Once it's over my head, I start to calm down. The episode has cost me very little distance, but it's left me feeling agitated. A mid-race change of clothes should be relaxed, but I've managed to make it a frantic affair. By the time I reach Jane again, she's fixed the pin. I'm still a bit grumpy but I'm calmer this time, even though I don't stop. The feeling of dry fabric against my skin is glorious.

Over the next lap, I start to regain my sense of humour. I can see that it might be funny to have your shirt pinned closed. Just not today.

18:04 FINDING WHAT WE'RE GOOD AT
44.74 MILES

I love running on the flat because it offers an easy rhythm that flows through the minutes and hours. I regularly run on canal towpaths and smooth river trails, and I do a lot of my faster training runs on the treadmill with the incline setting on zero. Flat landscape takes practice. The lack of variation in movement and effort can wreak havoc on unsuspecting bodies and minds. Racing on the flat rewards intelligent and consistent pacing. There's nowhere to hide; no steep inclines to walk and no downs to keep me going.

At first, I associated ultrarunning with mountains and was sure that my greatest moments would be in mountainous terrain. I love running in beautiful places, which in many parts of the world has included mountains. Long climbs, hard-won views and dusty legs, scratched and shaking from the relentless descent.

But most of my memories of running in the mountains are of putting on my running belt and heading off by myself. Rather than competing, those runs have been about the beauty of the landscape and the sense of adventure that comes from using your feet to cover the ground. For the past five years, my ankles have made trail running difficult – every uneven landing is painful, so it's only when I'm by myself and in less of a hurry that I can choose my foot placings more carefully. Maybe one day I'll be able to sort out my ankles enough to get stronger on the slopes, improve my technique and have a full go at the mountain ultramarathons. Perhaps I could even become as brave as their runners are about the inevitable falls.

I greatly admire the elite fell runners – their work rate going up the slopes and their skill on the hair-raising descents is a wonder to behold. Similarly, the short-trail and mountain runners. It would be nice to think I could do it just as well, but those runners are an entirely different breed.

Ultimately, my physiology is not that of an elite mountain runner. In lab tests, my running economy is unusually good, which means that I can run at a certain speed with less oxygen than most people. However, my VO2 Max (the rate at which I can process oxygen) is unexceptional for an athlete, so I don't process a large amount of oxygen at once. My economy helps to make up for this, but when it comes to running at very high speeds or blasting up a mountain, I will likely come off second best.

Economy and efficiency are useful for running a long way, though. Barely lifting my feet off the ground may be a recipe for disaster on a rocky path, but it is a boon for saving energy on a flat road or track.

Accepting the fact that flat and long runs suit me gives me the chance to make the most of my natural talents. I can run in the mountains for the joy of it and choose to compete on the flat because it's where I excel.

It's a gift to know what we are good at, but to get there sometimes means taking chances and trying new things. It can be easier to stick with what we know because it is safe – it won't risk failure or embarrassment, and it won't force us to ask whether we have gone as far as is possible on our current path. We don't lose anything by trying new things, and a new challenge might reveal a talent or passion we could never have imagined.

Flat and long is good for me – at least for now.

18:22 THE POWER OF PATIENCE
46.97 MILES

The temptation to do something different is immense. To speed up or to slow down. To stop or to walk. To force a result, to demand an outcome. But the only thing that will guarantee the outcome I need is to keep on doing what I'm already doing, for twenty-four hours. To keep on until the end.

To run faster will not get me to the end sooner: the finishing line is at twenty-four hours and running too fast, even for a little while, risks a catastrophic blow-up long before the finish. To walk or slow down too much will leave me short of the distance that I need to achieve or will precipitate a crisis of belief and an invitation to lose hope and give up.

I must simply do *this*. The time and the distance will take care of themselves. Sometimes the achievement is in resisting the need to force a change for as long as it takes to reach a goal.

18:33 MORE TIME THAN YOU THINK
48.22 MILES

'You always have more time than you think.' It's something my father told me years ago, before one of my first races, and it's come to be a mantra I use when things aren't going to plan. It can be too easy to think *my goal is lost* and so quit. In reality, the time you lose is rarely as important as you think. If you persist and do the best you can, it's often amazing what is still achievable. If you have to walk, then walk with intent and run as much as possible. If you slow down, then keep running as best you can. A result to be proud of is still achievable, and it is often surprisingly close to the original goal.

I once picked up an injury on one of the early hills of the Comrades Marathon. I couldn't run normally and with 45 miles ahead, my immediate concern was making the twelve-hour cut-off, after which no one is allowed to cross the finishing line. Things got worse when I vomited just before halfway – probably because I'd got myself into such an anxious state over the injury. On the upside, by then I was confident I could finish and was thinking that a time of under eleven hours would be possible, even if I carried on being sick.

I pressed on, resisting the temptation to sit or lie down as the dehydration got worse or I felt ill. As I moved through the course, I kept recalculating what was possible; ten hours, nine and a half, then nine. Eventually, to my shock, I finished in under eight hours – a lot slower than I had set out to achieve but a lot faster than what I thought was possible when my trouble started. I'm as proud of that run as any because of what I had to deal with to get that result.

You have more time than you think. These words are written in my race notes and I know Jane will also remind me of them if things go significantly off-plan. When something goes wrong, it's important not to panic and to take the time to think things through. As a friend who was in the Army says, 'The first thing to do if you are lost is to sit down.' It's equally important that my crew relax, think and then act with reason. If they can't get me to drink anything on one lap, they'll figure something out by the next one, or the one after that. And when they've come up with a good idea, they'll know where to find me.

18:41 THOSE WHO ARE POSITIVE
49.21 MILES

I told my family and friends about my dream to get an international vest years before it actually happened. The first person in my running club I talked to about it was my friend Julian Ferraro. He and I met in the final mile of the London Marathon many years ago. We were both wearing London Heathside running club vests and racing down Birdcage Walk towards Buckingham Palace. The friendly rivalry between clubmates often leads to the hardest racing; I overtook him, then he overtook me, and as I came back alongside him, we managed to smile, introduce ourselves and run to the finishing line together. It was a memorable way to meet.

Some years later, we were talking about my attempt to be selected for England over 100km and he said matter-of-factly, 'You can run sixty-two miles at seven minutes a mile.' Funnily enough, that's exactly what I would do five years later in the British 100km Championships. Another time, I had already run 10 miles before the start of the club's 20-mile run one Sunday and towards the end of it, Julian said, 'If this is you at thirty miles, it's really impressive.' I remember those moments clearly because of how much I valued his opinion.

A couple of years ago, I bumped into Gavin Evans, another long-time clubmate, in a park in London. I had just started being coached by Norm, and I told him about my two-year plan, which ends with this race today. 'That's amazing!' he said. He knew I hadn't achieved my goal yet, but he was excited for me because of what I was trying to do, and his genuine positivity suggested that he thought I might do it.

We listen for the cues that give us self-belief all the time, whether from parents, friends, partners, managers or coaches. To be surrounded by people who build us up and want us to be happy is one of the greatest gifts in life. To voice ambitious goals out loud can leave us feeling immodest or open to ridicule, but I suppose it all depends on who you tell.

The thing about the family and friends I told is that, whether they believed I could achieve my goal or not, they wanted me to believe that I could. No one laughed or tried to undermine me when it looked like it wasn't going to happen.

Some people make us feel good about ourselves and then others simply don't. At the far end of the spectrum are those who actively try to make us feel worse, often because of how bad they feel about themselves. The people we need in our lives are the ones who want us to be happy. They may not always know exactly the right thing to say, but they will always try to help us bring out the best in ourselves. They are prepared to listen, encourage and respect us for trying, whether we are successful or not.

18:51 ECCENTRICS AND CRAZIES
50.45 MILES

The first time I read about 24-hour races, they sounded mad. In an attempt to run for such a long time, surely most of it would be spent walking? And who in their right mind would want to run endlessly around a short loop? It was obviously little more than an event for eccentrics and crazies.

A few years later, as I started to think beyond the 56 miles of the Comrades Marathon and to research 100-mile races, the 24-hour one kept coming up. Many of the best 100-mile athletes in the world had run 24-hour races, both for the unique challenge and the opportunity to represent their country in major championships. Athletes I had read about for years, like Scott Jurek and the former 100-mile world record holder Don Ritchie, had participated in them. The more I read, the more intriguing the idea became.

A lot of ultrarunners talk about the 24-hour event as a 'pure' form of racing. It is just you and the track with nowhere to hide, both literally and figuratively. Even if you win, you finish at the same time as everyone else. There's no variation in elevation or scenery, and no course to navigate. The event is long enough that intelligent pacing is crucial, and short enough that you have to run relatively quickly the entire time. You will never spend the race hidden in the pack or disappear alone up ahead; each runner is as visible as any other. The race is running stripped of everything but you, time and what you are capable of doing with it.

Over the past few years, I've found the race reports of the current GB team and other athletes around the world increasingly compelling. The 24-hour race seems less an act of madness than a rite of passage for the ultrarunner embracing longer distances and interested in the purity of running. I've seen what others have done and have decided that it is possible for me too. The more you understand something, the less alien it becomes. Or maybe I've simply descended into the realm of the eccentrics and crazies.

19:04 SELF-TRANSCENDENCE
51.94 MILES

The official name of this race is the Self-Transcendence 24-Hour Track Race, but what is self-transcendence, and will I find it here? It sounds meditational, as if by running far enough I'll transcend my current state of consciousness and glimpse enlightenment, but that's not it. According to the race programme, self-transcendence is about progressing by striving to beat the current best *you*, rather than trying to beat everyone else. In other words, it's about focusing on becoming better yourself instead of measuring yourself against others.

Sri Chinmoy founded the Sri Chinmoy Marathon Team, who organise this race. He was a spiritual teacher and athlete who competed in a spirit of self-transcendence, which meant competing *with* rather than *against* other athletes. Achieving a new personal best was a source of joy, whether that meant an improved athletic performance or an achievement of character, like encouraging others or handling a loss gracefully.

My understanding of self-transcendence is inexpert, but I like the sense it has of moving forwards. It sounds a lot like the spirit of ultrarunning: the encouragement between athletes, the selfless giving way to others in races such as this and the personal struggle we're engaged in against our own minds and bodies. In races as long as this one, no one wins by being simply faster than someone else; so much can go wrong that where we finish is also a product of good or bad fortune and whether we are able to overcome our battle with ourselves.

I want to win this race, but achieving the British selection standard is far more important. If I come second and still make the standard, I'll be happy. And whatever happens, I know I'll be happy as long as I give everything I can. I hope there's a bit of the spirit of self-transcendence in that.

19:35 TEAM
55.42 MILES

My crew have dug in for a long night. For the first few laps, they applauded as I passed, and then we settled into watching each other from our parallel worlds. On most laps, I'm aware of them without looking specifically at what they are doing. When a feed is approaching, I look more carefully, wondering what I am about to be given and who is going to give it to me.

When one of them crosses the inner field or appears somewhere unexpected around the track, I find myself trying to figure out what they're doing. The only one who never seems to move is Norm's wife, Anne. Today is their wedding anniversary, and what could be better than this for a celebratory evening out? She sits under the gazebo in her fold-up chair, a pad of paper on her lap. She has a task of immense concentration and selflessness: she is my personal lap counter for the entire twenty-four hours and is recording every lap and split time. If things go to plan, she'll need to do this over 600 times.

She and Norm have organised, officiated and crewed many races, and know from experience to plan for the unexpected. My laps are being counted by the official human counters and by the electronic timing system, but Norm and Anne know that humans can make errors and electronic systems can break down, especially in weather conditions like these. With Anne's record, we can prove my performance if the other systems fail. It's an insurance policy that is under the full control of our team. It may seem like overkill but strange things do happen, and a failure to log even one lap could be the difference between making the selection standard or missing it, or between winning and losing the race. In a race from A to B it's obvious who's in the lead, but here it's a lot harder to tell and we can't just come back next week and try again – we'll lose a year if things don't work out this weekend.

When I saw other runners' supporters getting dinner from the race organisers' kitchen, I wondered whether my team had got theirs – after all, it's an endurance event for them too, and they'll need to look after themselves. They will get tired, wet and cold, and just like me they will have moments when they doubt the race will ever end. They will also worry about how I'm doing, especially Jane, for whom the whole event will be extremely stressful. But I know I can't afford to worry about them. I brought everything I could think of to make them as comfortable as possible, and now they need to look after themselves.

Helen and Rob are two of our closest friends and will provide backup and emotional support for Jane. They joined her to crew for me at my first 100-mile race – in which Rob also ran the last 22 miles with me as a pacer – and have travelled with us to South Africa a few times for the Comrades Marathon. Jane will have a complete picture of everything that happens during the race and will make decisions about what I need – their job is to help her in any way they can.

My friend Toby has been here for hours and will be back tomorrow. He is a natural cheerleader and I know that his reappearance will brighten my crew's morning at least as much as my own.

Then there is Norm, my coach, whose judgement and support will be invaluable to Jane. I know he is monitoring my progress but will not try to manage it – he will only intervene if he thinks I'm making a mistake, like going off too fast. So far he has been quiet, except to occasionally say, 'Well done, Mike.' His silence gives me confidence that I am doing the right things.

I could get to the end of twenty-four hours by myself, but I don't think I would run nearly as far. And it would be a much less rewarding experience if I wasn't sharing it with people I care about, especially Jane. I've heard people say that having your own crew in a long ultra helps by as much as 10 per cent, but I think it depends a lot on the athlete, the event and the crew themselves.

Having a crew is not always helpful – they can cost a runner a lot of time or distance, or even their race. A partner who is worried about the exhausted state of their loved one is much more likely to provide a way out for the athlete than a volunteer behind the organiser's food table who has no emotional attachment to them and has seen it all before. A runner who is already on the edge may crumble in the face of familiarity, in a similar way to the child who is hurt but toughs it out and then bursts into tears at the first sight of a parent. And then there are the bad crews, who might actively lobby for their athlete to drop out by complaining about their own discomfort or lack of sleep. It is much better to have no crew at all than to have a bad one.

When a crew is good, they can be hugely helpful to the runner. Everything is available when it is needed, time is saved, moral support given, and someone is thinking clearly when the athlete no longer can. However, there needs to be a clear plan. My team have an eating plan that details what I want, when I want it – although they will use their judgement. They also have a crew note detailing everything I think they need to know, from what I am aiming to achieve to tips on what to say when things get hard. I have tried to give them as much insight as possible into how I might be feeling, what I might be thinking and what might help.

The crew note reminds everyone that I will not be leaving the track before the twenty-four hours are finished, unless my life or long-term health are at risk or I have an injury so severe that it is not physically possible to keep moving forward. Otherwise, no amount of pain, illness or exhaustion will stop me. This understanding is essential, as it creates the context for how the crew will respond to me as things get difficult.

These special people have given up two days of their lives, and a night of sleep, to help me. I know that I'm fortunate to have this kind of support. I don't look at them as I pass again; my heightened awareness of them suddenly makes me feel self-conscious. As the hours pass, they will eat, drink, rest, talk, worry and plan. And I will run. Our parallel worlds will continue, touching only when I eat, every half-hour.

PART THREE

20:00 TO 23:59

20:06 ENDURANCE
59.15 MILES

My friend Ruth Storm doesn't call herself an adventurer, but it's hard to think of a better word to describe her. She does things like pull a sled unsupported from the edge of Antarctica to the South Pole, climb hard-to-reach mountains and cycle the Silk Route from end to end.

She and I are both endurance athletes, but our events are completely different. She ekes out her resources over weeks or months, somehow managing to sleep in extreme weather and enduring months of living in difficult circumstances. One of her many talents is the gift of being able to sleep in strange places. She is willing to live in discomfort for long periods, away from the luxuries of modern life. She has a social and cultural fearlessness, and the duration of her adventures is part of the appeal because of the richness of what it allows her to discover.

My events are about putting everything I have into one short period of time. For someone cycling the Silk Route, twenty-four hours is nothing, but I won't be able to spend another twenty-four hours at the same level of intensity for at least six months, and probably a year. My training is often arduous and I will be tired for months at a time, but at night I have my comfortable bed, a warm shower and as much food as my body needs. I have modern luxuries on tap, whereas Ruth can spend three months sleeping in a tent.

Humans have an amazing capacity to endure difficulty. Long-term illness. The loss of someone we love. The anxiety and fears of everyday life. The job we hate or the long commute. And then we voluntarily take on physical and mental challenges that make life even harder. Perhaps the willingness to face difficulty is part of what makes us human. Maybe when we take on a challenge, we are acting on the instinctive belief that positive outcomes will flow from hard effort. And maybe there's comfort to be found from difficulty that is within our control. Above all else, being challenged makes us feel alive, and we know that the harder we have to work for something, the more we will appreciate it.

Endurance is also a skill; as circumstances in our lives change, difficulty that was once unthinkable can become the new normal. We learn, adapt and keep pressing on. What I'm doing today would have been impossible for me fifteen years ago – not just for the lack of physical adaptation, but for my inexperience at this kind of endurance. The next time I do this, maybe it will be easier.

20:19 FAILING
60.64 MILES

I've only ever dropped out of one race. It was many years ago, at the London Marathon. I had started fast – too fast. I was wobbling on the tightrope between the ultimate performance and a crashing failure from early on, but the margins at the extreme edges of personal performance are fine and the tightrope wobbling doesn't mean you'll fall.

I was used to suffering in races from early on but knew that something wasn't quite right. I hung on for several miles and suddenly found myself standing on the side of the road, my race over. Dropping out had been unthinkable, but there I was. I was uninjured and could have carried on and run a good time, but I didn't want that – I wanted to be better than I'd been before and to run the kind of time that I knew I could. Everything else was irrelevant.

In the aftermath of the race, I learned how horrible it feels to drop out, and I hope I never have to do it again. I'd rather hobble to the finish or endure any pain than quit and suffer the horrible feelings of separateness from the race, from the experience of the other athletes and from the months of preparation – the terrible feeling of being left behind.

In ultras it's a bit different. So much can go wrong that longer events often have drop-out rates of more than 30 per cent. There can be good reasons for dropping out, including a risk of long-term harm or even death. To carry on in the face of persistent vomiting, diarrhoea or injury can be mindless rather than brave, and it can be hard to tell the difference at the time; at some point, we will all get it wrong. Every ultrarunner knows that the decision to drop out is never taken easily.

What *is* a failure? Any event in which I do my best may be a disappointment, but that doesn't mean it's a failure. I've looked back on performances and felt I should have done better, but I know I always do my best in a major race. If the result falls short of my expectations, it will be because my expectations were too high for my fitness level or the conditions on the day. In the past few years, even though I've improved as a runner, I've been disappointed in my performances at the Comrades Marathon. Most of my training, however, is on the flat to prepare me for races like today, not for the huge hills of Comrades. I might be a bit disappointed when I'm not as quick as I'd like to have been, but I know I've run well in the circumstances. It hasn't been a failure.

When I stepped off the road at the London Marathon, it was a failure because I could have carried on, but didn't because I had no other goals to fall back on when it was clear I wouldn't achieve my main one. It was also a failure that I lacked the humility to accept a subpar performance.

However, it is too easy to run to the same plan time and again and end up with a similar outcome. On that day, I put everything on the line to go for the big prize. It didn't pay off that day, but on others it has. You don't find the edge of your ability without falling off it occasionally. To go to the edge takes courage and sometimes we have to accept a fall with courage, too. There's no failure in that.

20:33 WHEN LEADERS SPEAK
62.14 MILES

My counter tells me I'm through 100km, a small but important milestone. The last time I ran this far was at the British 100km Championships earlier in the year. About halfway through that race, I ran past the GB 24-hour team manager, John Pares.

'Twenty-four-hour next year, Mike,' he called out.

John Pares is here watching me run, and he thinks I could be in his team one day. What a boost I got from those words in the middle of a tough race!

Leaders often underestimate the power of their words, but a handful of the thousands they speak on any given day could be the most important thing that someone hears all year. It could be as simple as some positive feedback or a thank you. It's often easier to say nothing. *What if I don't say the right thing? Why would anyone want to hear from* me? But I've seen the look on the face of someone when the CEO says hello to them; it gives them the value of recognition and respect. Sometimes when leaders speak, they will say exactly the right thing at the right time, even if they don't know it.

20:41 CONSTRUCTING NEGATIVES
63.13 MILES

I've been looking forward to this race. Years ago I used to dread them. For months beforehand, my body would flood with adrenaline and I'd have a feeling in the pit of my stomach that something terrible was going to happen. That's when I decided to visit the mental performance coach Andy Barton.

Andy asked me to imagine a race and to describe the light. *Dingy, grainy, with grey, leaden skies.* 'And the running?' *Strained, hard. There's suffering and tension.*

'If the scene is a movie, what's the theme tune?' he asked. *It's heavy and dark, epic. It's all about the struggle against the odds and the need to overcome.*

'Why can't it be "Walking on Sunshine?"' he asked, pointing out the words I used when I talked to him about racing and how almost everything I said about it was framed in negative terms.

He told me that the subconscious isn't good at humour, so when at the end of a race you say to your friend, with a smile, 'That was terrible,' your brain hears only that last word. We're very good at remembering negatives, he said – an instinctive talent that is useful for avoiding danger. If five good things and five bad things happen, we will likely remember all the bad ones and perhaps only one of the good. This makes it easy to build up a negative perception of something, whether an event, ourselves or racing. As far as my brain was concerned, racing was a terrible thing that I had to survive and overcome. I had to either give up racing or change the way I thought.

Now you'll hear me say that I'm really looking forward to the race, and it will be true. At first it wasn't, but saying it started to change the way I thought. When I imagine the big day, the picture is bright and I can feel myself smiling. My running is relaxed and smooth. I think how grateful I am to be running, how I'm there because I want to be and how well it is going.

I think about races during happy, upbeat songs and try to rein in negative thoughts and statements to stop myself from falling back into bad habits. Andy taught me the power of the word 'but' to negate what has gone before it and how we can use it to negate the negative things we find ourselves saying. It's worth a try, especially for those who beat themselves up with negativity. 'Oh, I'm so useless, *but* I'm going to learn.'

The race is going to be tough, *but* I'm prepared and I know it's something I can handle. Bring it on.

20:55 THE AMATEUR PROFESSIONAL
64.87 MILES

I used to avoid asking for help, but life got a lot easier when I realised that no one can know or do everything. A couple of years ago, I decided that not being a professional athlete needn't stop me from behaving like one.

A regular visit to the physio could help me catch problems early, even if daily treatment wasn't an option. A trip to my GP could give me insight into my iron and vitamin levels. Being tested in a university lab, just as a professional would be, gave me a good overview of my physiology.

A sports psychologist need not be the preserve of the professional, yet if your budget cannot stretch to a session, there are some good books and websites to draw from. Similarly, meticulous race planning is free of charge, as is taking the time to apply our minds and understand what did and didn't work. An informed sounding board can be found in the right coach or even simply a fellow runner; someone else whose opinion we respect.

For me, professionalism suggests a constant quest for improvement. It is a mindset; a desire to improve and an awareness that you can. When I am at a major race and see another competitor who is in some way better prepared than me (and this happens without fail), it is both a reminder and an impetus for me to become just that little bit more professional.

21:04 BAD PATCHES
65.86 MILES

This is really hard. The tiredness, manageable a minute ago, is suddenly shouting at me to stop. I should feel better than this. It shouldn't feel this hard so early in the race. *How can I possibly get to the end?*

It's like a switch has just brought the battle from the background of my consciousness to the foreground. I had it under control and suddenly I'm only just hanging on. It's a *bad patch* and all athletes are familiar with them. For some reason, the difficulty is suddenly magnified, but after a while, things improve and go back to how they were before the patch started.

The cause is often a mystery. The difficulty sneaks up on you. Bad patches have spelt the end of innumerable dreams. They mean the race favourite drifting from the back of the leading pack, the athlete dropping out 5 miles short of the 100-mile finish or the highly experienced runner shocked to be walking so early in their race.

The key is to spot a bad patch fast enough and to remember that it will pass. *This is just a bad patch. I will feel better in a while.*

The body goes through periods of feeling stronger or weaker. There's no linear decline, so there's always the hope that you will feel better later. On training runs, I often feel better in the second hour than I do in the first, or in the fourth than in the third. Those wonderful moments when everything just seems to work also have their shadow, when movement is deliberate and the air around the legs feels thick like toffee.

But mainly it is in the mind. I was once approaching halfway at the Comrades Marathon. I was at the start of an incline and I thought, *I'm not even halfway, I should feel better than this.* I instantly went from feeling tired but in control, to finding myself battling not to walk. I was taken by surprise, and the race became a struggle. When I reached that same point a couple of years later, I was prepared. I had run more than a marathon, mostly uphill, and feeling a bit tired was understandable. It meant I was running to plan, and that time there was no sudden worry to pierce my mental armour.

Athletes build up a memory bank of all the bad patches they have successfully navigated that they can draw on when things are difficult. Mental toughness is not just the willingness to face a challenge but also the belief that you can come out the other side. Coming through a lot of bad patches turns athletes into optimists.

In life there are those moments when the thing we want to do seems suddenly harder, when the piece of work that was challenging and exciting in an instant feels impossible or doomed to fail, or when a life dream seems suddenly out of reach.

These are moments of mental fragility, when confidence dips – whether because of the work of our own mind or the thoughtless words of someone else. Instead of giving up, it is worth carrying on for a while to see if we feel the same way later. It might just be a bad patch.

21:38 RECOGNITION
69.59 MILES

I see them in one frame, in front of me for just a moment before they spread out again. Geoff Oliver, Ann Bath and Marco Consani. Two of them are holders of world records who have helped to redefine our society's perceptions of ageing. One of them is a world-class international, though you are unlikely to ever see his easy motion on television. And all three of them are far from household names.

When I was a child, I went on holiday with my family to the Drakensberg Mountains. My father was an excellent runner, having competed in the steeplechase at the National Athletics Championships and completed the 56-mile Comrades Marathon, and during our trip he had hiked to the summit of the main mountain in the area. One day we were talking to another family in the hotel, and the father was telling us about a walk he'd been on earlier in the day to halfway up the mountain. His family gasped as if he had just climbed Everest. Then he let us in on his fitness secret: his running. Yet his achievements were clearly significantly below those of my father.

As I listened to him, I became increasingly frustrated. Didn't this man know who he was talking to? Surely my dad would set the record straight and mention his own achievements. Instead, he politely listened and made encouraging remarks as the man continued. Some onlookers joined the conversation – more people who were oblivious to my dad's achievements. I found myself getting more and more upset.

Eventually, it was over and the other family left. I turned

to my father, tears of frustration in my eyes. 'Why didn't you tell them that you went to the top of the mountain?' I asked. 'None of them know.'

'That doesn't matter,' he said, 'because *I* know.'

21:47 HAVING YOUR OWN EXPERIENCE
70.83 MILES

Back when I was a student, I read a book about trekking in the Himalayas and the idea of walking to Everest Base Camp completely captured my imagination. The description of the route and grainy photos of teahouses, Marxist revolutionaries and high-altitude paths seemed exotic and inaccessible. How wonderful it would be to walk that path!

Many years later, Jane and I decided to do that trek and began to find out more online and from a tour company offering guides and itineraries. One of my concerns was the potential for crowds – the trek has become incredibly popular and walking among crowds is not my idea of what being in the mountains should be like. I spent a lot of time doing research to try to get a feel for just how bad it could be, and whether we should go.

In the end, we went ahead and booked it, but I continued to worry. Would I spend the whole trip annoyed? Would the route be one long trail of sweet papers and cigarette butts? Then I came upon a website that described every bit of the walk, with photos of each section of path. I started to read, feeling my mood rise or sink depending on what each page revealed.

Then a thought hit me right between the eyes: *what am I doing?* In the modern world, there are fewer and fewer places left unreviewed. Photos and recommendations are so often a precursor to arriving somewhere that we deprive ourselves of surprise and wonder; in my concern about something I was unable to control, I was taking this to the extreme. Once I'd accepted that there would be plenty of other hikers on the trek, I was able to enjoy the trip for what it was – a walk in an incredibly beautiful and interesting place. At each turn, there were things we'd never seen before, and we opened our minds to whatever the experience had to offer. The other walkers were part of that, and I found moments of tranquillity by going for runs on quieter paths or by retracing our route later in the day.

Before my first 100-mile race, I learned a lot from other runners' race reports and advice, though some of the stories made the distance seem even more daunting. Hallucinations, illness, falls, injuries, chronic dehydration, irresistible sleepiness and hypothermia seemed common. Was I going to hallucinate or spend hours sitting exhausted in aid stations? Maybe, but the only way I would find out was by running. And while it was useful to understand what *could* happen, it was even more useful to think about what I could do to prevent those things happening to me. My objective should be to make my stories as boring as possible – if my race were a trip to the Arctic, I would be the dull explorer who *didn't* fall through the ice.

To be prepared for an extreme scenario is important but should not be confused with expecting it to happen. It's the same on this track. Before the race, I learned so much from other people who have been here before, but the lines of my lane have not yet begun to form strange shapes as they have for some runners over the years, nor have I yet seen anyone running beside me other than those I know are real. That doesn't mean it cannot happen, it's just that I don't expect it to. With this mindset, I'm not looking for the first signs of madness and worrying about when it might come.

I have enough challenges in my own experience of these hours. And when the race is done, I'll have something to share that others might find helpful before finding their own way.

22:01 FOOD
72.33 MILES

My eating plan for the race has gone out the window. Jane handed me a gel and I could tell just by looking at it that there was going to be a problem. I manage to swallow it but know that it's the last gel I'll be having in this race. The nausea has been creeping up on me over the past hour, which is really disappointing, given the effort I've put in to figuring out what to eat during a race. I'd hoped that more solid food, like bread and energy bars, in between the gels and drinks would stop it coming on, but that hasn't worked.

I hope there will be some food I can tolerate as the night goes on, or my race will be over. How much I will need I don't know yet – everyone talks about getting 200–300 calories an hour, but I suspect I can get by on a lot less. For me, the worry is getting something into my system that will keep my blood sugar level up.

I don't come from a family of adventurous eaters and I took that philosophy into adulthood. In my twenties, I ate only because we all have to. I found little joy in food, except for chocolate. There was no rationale for most of the things I refused to eat, apart from red meat, which I had given up because of animal welfare. Dinners and parties were about drinking rather than eating. At a restaurant, the eating felt like a chore to be ticked off – it was not why I was there, and on many occasions I'd happily have not eaten at all. At a party, if no one put a plate of food in front of me, I often wouldn't get around to eating anything.

There were exceptions: the vegetable stew and pitta bread

I ate at a hostel while travelling, the junk food that soothed a hangover, the special meal that someone made for me. One night in my mid-twenties, I was feeling so unhealthy that I went to a restaurant and binged on the salad bar. *I could try to live like this*, I thought. *Eating and enjoying real food and looking after myself.* I remember it clearly because it was like an epiphany. But I never went back.

When I met Jane, if she was cooking, she wouldn't tell me what we were having. I started to enjoy some of the things that I thought I didn't eat, and as my assumptions were tested, the barriers began to fall. Now I eat anything, provided it's vegetarian. My relationship with food is still a work in progress, but now I enjoy food for its own sake and actively seek out what will make me feel healthy and a better athlete.

I know that our relationship with food is complex. There are many reasons why we eat the way we do. Part of it is age – when we are young, we often eat like we might live forever, and when we're older, we eat like we'd prefer to decide how long we might live for. And then there's the correlation between how we eat and how we feel – about our lives and about ourselves. I feel worthy of those salads now.

In ultrarunning, there's a lot of talk about 'nutrition', but I don't use that word myself; it sounds too much like 'healthy eating'. Sugary drinks and gels may have their place in racing, but I don't want to confuse them with something that might be good for me. Perhaps it is different for those who manage to stick to healthy food while racing.

I worry when I see people at the gym follow a short, low-intensity workout with gulping down a sports drink, say, and a protein bar. Someone has convinced them that this is what athletes do. But it means they end up taking in more calories than they burn, and gain weight. Then they might stop exercise because they think it doesn't work.

There's a lot of hype around 'fuelling'. When I started eating less during marathons, it had no negative impact on my performance – I needed something, but not very much. If I could run 20 miles in training on a few gulps of water, I realised I shouldn't need a lot of gels and drinks to race just a few miles further, even at a much faster pace.

When I stopped carbo-loading before marathons, I felt much better. Normal eating gives me everything I need for the race, given how inactive I am in the final few days. I don't carbo-load before racing 100 miles, either. I just make sure to eat well. And that's the approach I've taken for this race.

When I'm asked about carbo-loading and eating, I always say that the best approach is to do whatever works for you. A gel that serves no physiological purpose is still worth eating if it provides a psychological boost.

Most of us buy into the hype around feeding to some degree. In training I can run fifty miles on an occasional drink of water and a few gels, whereas in this race I've been trying to cram the equivalent in calories of two gels down my throat every hour. At fifty miles, I'd had the equivalent of about thirteen gels, and yet I'm running slower now than during a training run. The thinking is that if you don't eat sooner you'll pay later, and while I'm sure there's plenty of truth in that, I suspect we are all different. It is probably a question of degree. I would prefer to follow my instincts and eat much more sparingly. After all, in addition to the carbs I ingest, I'm carrying enough fat to last for weeks. But when am I going to test the theory? Now? In a year's time at the world championships? It feels safer to stick with the eating dogma, even if it doesn't quite stack up.

What is healthy food, anyway? It's changing all the time. I was raised on margarine but that now seems to have been a terrible mistake. We are told that food with lots of fat either kills you or saves you. Carbs are good or bad depending on who you talk to, just as there is always a fashionable new superfood that is either elixir or snake oil.

Maybe it just depends on who we are – if we listen to our bodies, we can tell what's good for us. We are all different in so many ways, so why not in how we react to different kinds of food?

So now it's down to what I can tolerate. I brought along almost anything I could think of, including my favourite sorts of crisps and chocolate. Neither of those appeals at all now, though. Let's see what Jane comes up with next.

22:22 THE THINGS WE DO FOR FRIENDS
74.81 MILES

We all bear scars from childhood and Helen, one of my crew, is no exception. The first time we met, she made me laugh with stories of the camping trips she'd been forced to go on with her parents. In all her memories, she was either outside in a pouring gale or huddled in a freezing tent. As a consequence, she has refused to go camping her entire adult life.

As I pass my crew, I look through the driving rain and see her face peering out of our tent – I can tell she has a long night ahead of her. Worse still, she does not particularly like running, preferring yoga and art. She doesn't need me to hand her a bottle in the middle of a yoga class, though I wish she did because then I'd be able to help her in return. Of course, I realise that she's helping because she wants to – it's just who she is.

I was amazed by how many friends offered to stand out here tonight. As I go past again, I can see Helen trying to move some water from the top of the sagging gazebo with a stick, while Rob is eating and watching us run around the track. Perhaps after another fourteen hours of watching us, Helen will become a running fan, too. Somehow, though, I doubt it.

The thing they are both giving tonight is time. I have come to understand that when it comes to generosity, time is the ultimate currency.

22:58 A SENSE OF MOVING FORWARD
78.79 MILES

Two and a half years ago, I started learning to play the piano. I've always admired people who can play musical instruments, and the idea that I could be one of them myself seemed incredible. Starting from scratch is always difficult, but when my laboured efforts seemed pointless, I imagined myself ten years later able to play. All I had to do was persevere on any given day and I would get there. Of course, I understand now that when that day comes, I'll look at my ability and, while I'll be proud of how far I have come, I will also understand how little skill I have compared to those I admire. But still, I'll have gone further than I ever imagined possible and I will continue to practise and make progress. *In five years' time*, I will say, *I'll be able to play the piano with real expression.*

I started to learn the piano a fortnight before I had an operation to have bone impingements removed from my ankle joints – I knew I was about to be on crutches for many weeks. The return to running was long and hard. After plenty of rehab in the gym, when I eventually managed a 20-yard jog I could still barely get my feet off the ground. It was a real shock.

There were moments when I doubted I'd ever be able to run well again. It was then that I was most grateful for having decided to learn the piano. It's always good to have something in life with which you feel you are moving forwards. I hope I carry this belief throughout my life. If I'm blessed to live to an old age, I plan to have some activity that enriches my life and at which I can get better each day.

When I thought about the operation, I knew it would be hard to take time away from running and feel my fitness ebb away. What if something went wrong? Or what if it all went fine but I never got back to the same level?

There would be months of pain, frustration and uncertainty, so running time became piano time. Most importantly, I had something in my life that enhanced my sense of self-worth; having the discipline to learn a new instrument was something I could be proud of, even if my identity as a runner was under threat. If things went badly, I could become a decent piano player instead of a decent runner, turning the page to a new chapter.

23:04 BEING COACHED
79.29 MILES

Norman stands at the side of the track in the rain, staring intently at something. As a former winner of the Berlin Marathon, a race organiser and a coach to international athletes, there can't be much he *hasn't* seen.

Still he stares, as if he's counting my steps. It wouldn't surprise me if he was. The idea that he's here just for me, that someone would travel across the country to stand in the rain overnight simply because I'm running, is almost strange.

For many years I was resistant to the idea of having a coach. I was an experienced runner and thought I knew my body better than anyone else ever could. *I coached myself*, as many athletes say, which is fine until you meet the person who can do a better job than you. Maybe coaching input is the same as any other kind of advice: it needs to come from the right person at the right time.

Some years ago, I realised I could find out how the elite runners trained by enlisting one of them as my coach. One of the great things about our sport is that there are some world-class ultrarunners who offer coaching. Of course, a good runner doesn't necessarily make a good coach, but Ian Sharman is both. He is one of the best and most consistent trail ultrarunners in the world and he also has a real passion for the Comrades Marathon, which was my main focus then. I quickly saw the value of fresh perspective and new ideas. After years of doing the same thing, I found it refreshing to do new training sessions that engaged both body and mind. Unfortunately, our time together was cut short when my ankles deteriorated to the point where consistent training became impossible.

Norm and I work collaboratively. Each week, I report the training I've done and he gives me a training schedule for the next week, based on his long-term plan. I tweak it as the week unfolds, taking into account the state of my body and the other demands on my time. I respect Norm's experience and knowledge, but he also trusts my own judgement – if it were any other way, it wouldn't work.

The best coaches don't just understand training – they understand people. Norm knows that different things motivate different people and that some athletes need almost daily input while others need considerably less. And he also knows how to build confidence and belief, which is the most valuable thing a coach can do. The best ones foster belief in the right goals – challenging but achievable ones, based on an understanding of the athlete's potential.

When I started working with Norm, my plan was clearly laid out: run for England at 100km and then for GB at 24-hour. We began to talk about *when* I was going to run for England, as if it were inevitable. What was once a dream became a given. My whole context changed, and I believed it because Norm believed it and I believed in him.

The athlete will be looking for any small cue from their coach, from a tone of voice or an offhand remark to supportive body language. A rousing pep talk before a race cannot make up for months of negativity. If the coach has been showing a lack of confidence in the athlete, a few positive words will not seem believable. The coach who rallies their team at half-time may come out with some great words, but they will be tapping into the trust they have built up over a period of months or years. When the coach says the team can do it, they believe it because of the credibility of everything else the coach has told them.

Norm is now walking in the direction of the timekeepers. There will be something he wants to check – he's not prepared to leave anything to chance. He loves the excitement of races and will be enjoying talking to his ultrarunning friends about what's going on. His passion for the sport is infectious and he's happy to be here, but I know the main reason he has travelled across the country for a long, sleepless night is his belief in me.

23:14 THE HUMAN BODY DOES NOT RESPECT CIRCUMSTANCE
80.53 MILES

I don't understand it. I'm hardly drinking anything as a result of the nausea and yet, less than an hour after I last went to the toilet, my stomach is tensed and cramping, and I feel a desperate need to pee. Running normally is impossible. Perhaps it's the cold and the rain, but the need is sudden and immediate.

The thought of being in the bathroom, out of the rain and standing still, is both wonderful and unwelcome. However, I don't have a choice and as I near the starting line, I run to the outside of the track and across the twenty or so metres to the toilet block. The relief is immediate, but it lasts just a couple of seconds before my head reels as my body tries to adapt to the sudden lack of movement. My breathing is loud in the quiet room. I can feel my wet clothes pressed to my skin in a way that I couldn't when I was outside. I'm conscious of every second that passes, each one a moment of respite with a terrible cost; the clock doesn't stop for this. The second I'm finished, I run back out, catching my reflection in the mirror; I look so gaunt and pale that I barely recognise myself.

My legs have begun to seize up during the break, and as I run across the track, everything is stiff and sore. It's a struggle to get moving normally again but I'm relieved to be back in the inside lane. The pain I can feel in my legs and hips starts to ease, as my brain accepts that the ordeal is not yet over.

The toilet break has probably cost me just over a minute; it's nothing really, but if it happens once every hour, the time will quickly start to add up. I can easily recall how good those first few seconds of rest felt, but it's the faintness, the anxiety and the pain of restarting I need to remember. Hopefully I won't need to go again for another few hours.

23:21 THE DARK
81.27 MILES

The power of the stadium lights is amazing. In the weeks leading up to the race, I wondered what would happen if the electricity at the track went out. Would the cars parked around the track switch on their headlights and have us running through an otherworldly fog of beams? I have three head torches in my kit in case of a power failure. How different my run would feel in a narrow beam of light.

It took me a while to get used to the idea of running with a torch. It started when my mother-in-law bought me one for my birthday, but it sat in a drawer until one day when I was struggling to drag myself out to train. I was trying to think of a new route to run, but then it came to me: maybe I didn't need somewhere new, because running in a nearby park would surely be very different in the dark? A little later, I turned away from the streetlights, switched on the torch and headed into the fields of Hampstead Heath.

I immediately felt as though I were in a bubble. I lost all sense of the city – all that existed was the beam of light and the darkness at its edges. Anxious not to trip, I stared at the rough ground just in front of me. My breath swirled eerily in the cold air. I felt blinded and vulnerable because of the lack of peripheral vision. Suddenly a huge dog appeared from the shadows and ran through the far reaches of my torchlight. In that moment I didn't know whether to be concerned for it or me, and then it was gone.

Eventually I started to relax. I ran better as I adjusted to the light of the torch and became less apprehensive about what might appear in the beam. I stopped in the middle of a wood and switched off the light for a minute to enjoy the novelty of the darkness, hearing and seeing more as my senses adjusted. As I approached Parliament Hill, I was surprised to meet people admiring the view of the city below, some of them walking with nothing but the ambient light. By the time I got home, it felt like I hadn't just been on a run – I'd been on an adventure.

Running in torchlight is normal for many ultrarunners, but I've not done it enough to get blasé and the sudden appearance of an animal or another runner is still remarkable to me. And then there's the utterly unexpected. One evening when I was nearing the end of a run, I decided to cut through some woods. As I ran down the hill, I was astonished to see a long row of lights where I knew there should be nothing but trees and darkness. I could hear the murmur of voices, and as I got closer I realised that the lights were lanterns being carried by children walking through the trees. When I reached them, a teacher explained that it was a 'lantern walk'. I can still feel the magic of the moment I first saw those lights.

Night means darkness, and darkness instinctively means danger. When I started running, it was months before I even ran under the streetlights – running was something you did during the day. Of course, much of this is a result of perspective, which can change.

A couple of months ago, I was sitting outside my tent on a Lakeland peak, enjoying the last of the evening light, when two hikers appeared on the path. It was a good two hours' walk down to the village and my immediate thought was that they must be in trouble. I started walking towards them but realised that they were calm and well kitted out. We exchanged a wave and I watched them disappear into the gloom. They were taking advantage of the remaining light to walk along the ridge, comfortable in the knowledge they could get down to the village under torchlight.

Woods can be eerie, the beam of the torch is modest and the dangers can be very real, especially in parks or wild places we are not familiar with. Caution after hours is necessary anywhere, in cities or the countryside, but with a good torch and some sound judgement, the darkness is an opportunity for new experience – an adventure in a parallel world that could be just yards away from home.

23:43 WHY?
83.76 MILES

Why? I've heard the question many times. It's not something I ask myself – I just have a certainty that I want to do it. Perhaps the need *is* the reason; but why then do I have the need?

When I hear about some feat of physical endurance, it normally feels obvious why the person is doing it. Why wouldn't they? Why wouldn't a swimmer swim across an immense body of water? Why wouldn't a climber climb an especially difficult mountain? Why wouldn't a cyclist want to test themselves day after day? I love hearing about these great feats and can relate to them; I sometimes wish it were me doing them.

There are so many reasons *why* that to choose just one neglects the others. It is my sport and I love the feeling of movement. There is the sense of achievement and of having got the most from myself. More recently, I've been running to earn the privilege of an international vest. With or without the vest, I always have the desire to win a race or achieve a new personal best or some other target. Then there is the mental wellbeing that flows from the effort, from the planning and the sense of purpose. The added richness that challenges bring to our lives, and the chance to see the world in a different way. The feeling of extreme physical fitness, and the sense of belonging and community.

Any of these is a reason for running, and there are others. But maybe the real answer is simply because it seems like a good idea – and that the only way to find out why, is to do it.

PART FOUR

24:00 TO 03:59

00:09 QUESTIONING LABELS
86.49 MILES

I only ran on a synthetic running track once during my school years. I was seventeen and it was my last race in a school vest. There had been a real sense of anticipation all season as we trained and raced on grass fields. The last race of the season would be different: if we won our local school league we would be running in a regional final at a university with a real all-weather athletics track.

We discussed the surface endlessly; how much faster would it be than the bumpy grass lanes we were used to? Would it be bouncy? Perhaps it would be impossible not to run faster on such a special surface.

Eventually the day came. The school took athletics seriously and hired a fleet of buses to transport hundreds of pupils to the stadium. I sat nervously in the stands with my classmates, waiting to warm up. My race was the 1500m, and our team of five had been unbeatable all season – on a couple of occasions we had finished first to fifth. I left my classmates, changed into my spikes and soon felt the rubbery surface of the track under my feet, stretching ahead of me magnificently. It felt fast.

We stood on the starting line. I was filled with adrenaline, though I knew the feelings of fright and weakness would soon turn into power. Three and three-quarter laps of the track awaited. I looked across the line of other runners and glanced up at the hundreds of spectators in the stand, trying not to let my nerves spoil the moment. This was it.

After the sharp blast of the gun, off we went. The pace of the race was like nothing I'd ever known. I breathed harder and moved faster than I had thought possible. Every second was agony and every step was the hardest I had ever run. After the longest four minutes of my life, I entered the finishing straight and made a final desperate effort that seemed to last forever. And then it was over. I lunged across the line, in last place.

I looked at my watch. I had done it – I had improved my personal best by sixteen seconds. Relief and joy flooded through me as I fought back tears. All the months of worry and stress were over – on the day that counted the most, I had been better than I had ever been. I walked over to my coach, still breathing heavily, and smiled. She nodded. It was less than I expected.

'My time!' I said. She looked at her clipboard and confirmed what I had captured on my watch, before turning away.

My time, I thought to myself, walking away. *My best ever. I did it.* I still felt slightly dazed from the effort and headed off to find my teammates and change into my tracksuit. Soon I was back in the stands, still flushed with pride and relief.

'What happened to you?' my classmates asked.

'Sorry?' I replied.

'You were last. What happened?'

'I ran a personal best – faster than I've ever run.'

'Oh, right.'

Everyone turned back towards the track – the relays were about to start.

And so I sat, the joy seeping out of me. I was no longer the competitor, the fastest I'd ever been. I was just Mike, who'd come last.

It's thirty-two years later and I'm aiming to run far enough in twenty-four hours to qualify to run for Great Britain.

Fifteen years ago, only having recently given up smoking, I watched the prize-giving at my local 10km race. I had done okay, though I had gone out too fast and finished somewhere around thirtieth. The lithe creatures walking onto the stage and collecting the cups were like a different species to me. *What must it feel like to walk up there and take home a trophy? To have crossed the finishing line with a thousand runners behind you?* I could ask the questions without envy or regret, because it simply wasn't a possibility for me. I had some natural ability but was not someone who could win races. I was a participant with modest goals and had always been that way, in school track and cross country. I understood my limitations.

At the same race some years later, I stepped onto the stage to shake the hand of the announcer. I had come third – a podium finish. While I was shocked to be up there, I felt I deserved it. It was the culmination of an incremental process of coming to believe that more was possible.

There's no shortage of runners who are surprised to discover that they can run faster or further than they thought possible, whether that's one mile or many more. Maybe it's because of how bad they felt at school cross country or because someone unkind had told them they weren't athletic. At least with running we can test our assumptions and redefine our expectations. We can reject the labels from childhood, and choose to follow the road or trail wherever it takes us.

What we believe we can do as runners relates to our preconception of our physical, athletic self, but what about everything else? Can we take this experience and apply it to the other labels we carry through our lives?

00:20 HEALTH
87.74 MILES

Running like this is not good for me. I don't need a magazine article or a medical paper to tell me that; it's pretty obvious. Pain, nausea, swelling, exhaustion, a partial shutdown of non-essential bodily functions – these things do not happen in healthy pastimes. But we runners did not turn up today to get some exercise. We are exceeding the recommended limits of vigorous activity by design rather than ignorance.

Although the racing isn't physically healthy, most of the training is, and racing at extreme intensity is an irregular occurrence. Every week, thousands of ultrarunners will participate in events at a far lower intensity – either training runs for those occasional all-out races or to enjoy a run with friends. Fifty miles will always be tiring and for many people it will be daunting, but for those who are used to it, it is not actually all that extreme.

Then there is the mind. After my first 100-mile race, for a few days I sometimes slurred my speech slightly. For about a week I struggled to find words or to think with clarity. Perhaps at some level these races also contain a sense of trauma: do our instincts really understand that we are racing voluntarily rather than fleeing from danger?

I had no such problems in training for that race, though, even after my longest training runs. And what a sense of purpose I have in the months before a target race! There's something so compelling about having a race to look forward to. The reading, learning and dreaming, and all that does to stimulate my brain. I was driven by the need to train, to get out from behind my computer into the world. The places I wouldn't otherwise have seen, the people, the changing seasons and the crisp light of a sunny winter's day. The sense of wellbeing in a park, a wood or a hidden space in the austere cityscape, and the sense of achievement and self-fulfilment that lasts for a lifetime compared to the physical or mental strain of a race.

The body and mind are a double act that is happiest and healthiest when engaged with life. On the face of it, today will do me no favours, but to pursue health at the expense of living is surely a sadly limited approach. This race is part of a lifestyle that has given me a greater sense of physical, mental and emotional wellbeing than I have had at any other point in my life. I am happy, and what could be healthier than happiness?

00:42 JANE
89.97 MILES

I met Jane while I was in Dublin on business. I was living in Johannesburg and she lived in London. In theory, a relationship was impossible, but after our first date the longest we went without seeing each other was a few weeks. I took major detours through London on business trips and she often flew out to Johannesburg, sometimes for just one night. She would fly on Friday night after work, land in Johannesburg on Saturday morning, fly back on Sunday night and go straight from the airport to her office on Monday morning.

Eventually, it became unsustainable and we decided we had to be in the same place, which when you live in separate countries normally means living together. It's incredible to me now, but at the time I was unable to make that commitment. However, Jane wasn't willing to let our relationship drift – we'd been together for a year and a half and if I couldn't commit to her, what hope did we have? We separated and I sat in Johannesburg for a few weeks, facing a future without her. I can remember exactly where I was standing when I realised the stupidity of my decision and it sank in that everything was empty and meaningless without her. But I had raised the stakes: Jane had been willing to live together, but I knew that it would now be all or nothing. To get her back, I'd have to ask her to marry me. But getting married was unthinkable, wasn't it?

I found a seat on a flight to London the following night and sent Jane a message asking if I could come and talk to her. She replied that she was willing to hear what I had to say. The next morning, I explained to my CEO that I had to travel unexpectedly. As I left his office, he put his hands on my shoulders and said, 'Good luck – I'm rooting for you.' Then I went to a jewellers to buy a ring. The shop assistant serving me said, 'She'll want to choose her own, so get her a ring when you come back together.' And in Jane's case she was absolutely right.

I arrived in London early the next morning and took a taxi straight to Jane's flat. When she opened the door, I was standing there with my suitcase. 'Well?' she asked. I told her there were things I needed to say, but that I was tired and grimy after the overnight flight and would like to have a shower first. 'No,' she said. 'What do you want to say?'

And so, standing in her kitchen, I told her how I'd been an idiot, which I suppose she already knew, and that life without her was deprived of meaning. And then I asked her to marry me, and she said yes. Later that evening, I told Jane that I must be the only person who ever proposed marriage so they could have a wash! We married five weeks later – we'd wasted enough time. We lived in Johannesburg for a short while and then made London our home.

Jane's primary concern is my happiness and mine is hers. Tonight I know it is difficult for her to watch as I tire. The races still worry her, though hopefully less than they did when this was all new. I remind her before each major event that I have the experience and know what I'm doing. She's a marathon runner too, and I know from supporting her how easy it is to worry. When you're competing in a race, you know you can win through, but when you're watching someone else run, you can only hope. When she races I'm a nervous wreck.

Jane is here to crew me and also to take care of me, which goes way beyond handing me a drink. If there's a problem, she wants to know about it. And if there's a decision to be made about my wellbeing, she wants to make it because she is the one who knows me best. She wants to be there for me, whatever that entails. In this case, it's standing for twenty-four hours in the rain, but I know she'd spend eternity there if that's what it took – and that I'd do the same for her.

01:16 HOME
93.70 MILES

Before the race, I received an email from Walter Hill, one of the British selectors and a former runner for Great Britain. He wrote, 'I know it might sound crazy but I always found the 24-Hours a euphoric experience. No emails or phone calls – just the delight of movement around a track which is your home for 24 hours.'

This positivity helped to allay my fears. His words conjured up a mental image of running alone on a track at night-time, a joyful acceptance of fatigue and a complete immersion in the experience. Given how much I love the sense of movement, to be able to run for so many hours is a rare opportunity that should be embraced.

I look around and make a conscious effort to take in the sights. The colour of the track, the lights bright above it and the trees. Sanctuary, comfort and familiarity. I feel at home. I force myself to smile, making the shape with my mouth. And again. It helps, if only for a moment.

I run, so I'm a runner. Mike the Runner. It has become part of my identity, intrinsic to who I am and how I'm perceived by others. But what if I no longer run? What if I become ill or injured or decide one day that I've simply had enough – who will I be then? Just Mike? Or Mike who used to run?

I was recently talking to someone at a party and they said, 'Oh, you're the runner.' I said, 'Yes, among other things.' I *am* the runner, but there's more to me than that.

To many friends I've made in recent years, running is central to how they see me. To older friends, my primary identity might be something I've carried from a different time of my life and the running is just another chapter. My newer friends still see me for who I am, but a major theme is there that wasn't fifteen years ago.

Identities are easy to pick up and hard to shed. I'm known in at least one house on our street as 'Lycra Guy', and I don't think that would change even if I burned my winter running tights and never ran again. My mother once said she liked penguins and she now has a lot of penguin figurines, none of which she bought herself.

In families, we can reinvent ourselves a hundred times and still be seen as something we were a lifetime ago. The young one or the naughty one. Our parents change too, but it can be hard to see them for what they have become and as their friends see them.

We are often defined at first glance by our job, a pastime or a passion that has led to a lifestyle choice. The vegan, the cyclist, the musician, the doctor or the wine buff. Of course, to someone who knows us in a different context, our identity might be different, but there's often a dominant theme.

When I was elected chairman of a global trade group, the demands of the role consumed me entirely. I was a spokesperson for the industry and found myself promoted as the face of the organisation. I achieved status and recognition, and was invited to speak all over the world in front of thousands of people, stayed in the best hotel suites, held press conferences and solved big problems. When my term of office ended, the Chairman still did those things, but I no longer did them. If I wasn't the Chairman, who was I? I was just thirty years old, but how could I top the things I had already done?

Any professional sportsperson who retires at a similar age would be able to relate to my situation. Retirement at any age brings a loss of status and identity, but for the young there is the additional fear of having already peaked with so much life still ahead. *Is everything else I do always going to be less than this?*

If I'd also been 'the Runner' when I was 'the Chairman', the transition would have been easier. If I had it to do again, I would find a way to invest more in other parts of my life, even though work was the dominant aspect of my identity.

Reinvention can be difficult, but it is possible at any point in life – it just takes courage and the willingness to do what makes us happy and feel fulfilled. In my case, I started to learn to pursue the things that made me happy rather than the things I thought I was supposed to want. I became the entrepreneur, the husband, the sportsman, the friend, the brother and the son. The reinvention was not like for like, it was one thing replaced by many as I exchanged focus for diversity. I am proud to have been the Chairman, but it is the perspective and experience it gave me that I value now rather than the status.

I suppose I am doing this the wrong way around. I have already had a successful career, and my aim now is to reach an elite level in sport. The unique nature of ultrarunning gives me that opportunity despite my age, but if it was not running, I hope it would have been some other reinvention towards whatever could make my life richer.

Who am I? For the moment, I'm fine being Mike the Runner. Among other things.

01:42 MUSIC
96.19 MILES

The jukebox in my head often repeats the same few lines of a song over and over. The repetition can be useful if the song suits the moment. Something rousing and inspiring might help at this point in the race, but as usual the DJ in my brain seems to be choosing tracks completely at random. What use do I have right now for the same few words from 'Carnival', a song by Natalie Merchant, about being lost inside her own mind? It's one of my favourite songs, but is this the time and place? If the universe has a voice, I think it probably sounds like Natalie Merchant, but what is it trying to tell me? Again and again, I hear the same line. And what I hear is not Natalie Merchant – it's me. But *is* it? Does the voice inside my head have its own voice?

Some runners have solved this problem by staying plugged into music for large parts of the race. My phone and headphones are with my crew, charged and ready to go – all I have to do is ask for them. And before the race I compiled a number of playlists. Would I want to be enlivened by 'London Fast'? Would I want to be introspective with 'London Mellow' or would I want to pass the time with 'London Long'? And why didn't I make a playlist called 'London Where the Fuck is Noon?'

Listening to music now would, I know, feel like an assault on my tired mind, a shouting match with the endless conversations inside my head. It has been the same at other races – I feel an active revulsion at the thought of music. It may have been different if I'd tried before I became so tired, but the thought had not occurred to me. Perhaps at the time I was just too lost inside my own mind? Perhaps the universe is laughing at me.

It is impossible to focus completely for twenty-four hours, but I have a natural inclination to concentrate on what I'm doing rather than to take my mind elsewhere – I find it's one of the keys to good performance, and so I constantly check in with the information my body is giving me and reflect on what I discover. Music would be an interruption rather than an enabler; one source of data too many.

Strangely, when I hit the treadmill for hard running sessions, I have music blaring in my ears and it definitely makes it easier, and several times a week I'll run with music just for the joy of it.

It's only on long runs that I never have music. They're my chance to process whatever's in my head without the constant external stimuli of messages, news, TV and music. It's the mental equivalent of sitting and reflecting, with the added benefit of exercise. How often do we just exist without looking at a smartphone or staring at a screen? How much time do we spend in silence, without TV, radio or music filling the void?

Maybe the arguments in my head would be soothed by the music, but I'm used to the sound of the voice in my head that starts the trouble. When it makes the case for stopping or walking, I've heard it all before. I've won the argument many times and know I can win it again, as long as I can spot it quickly and hear it for what it is.

One thing about being 'lost inside my own mind' is how quickly it passes the time. Perhaps the universe is on my side after all.

02:17 TRAVELLING FAR WITHOUT DISTANCE
100 MILES

Norm is standing with Adrian Stott, the official race timekeeper, on the inside of the track. They are deep in conversation and studying a piece of paper. I've passed them a few times already, and I know they're here because I'm close to reaching 100 miles – they'll record the time of those of us who make it that far during the race.

They don't say anything as I pass them and my heart sinks a little – being in sight of such a major milestone is making me conscious of distance and time in a way that I could do without. Looking out for something makes each lap seem longer, each step too important. It's impossible to lose yourself in the rhythm of running when each lap could herald the arrival of 100 miles.

My plan had been to get to that point between fourteen and fifteen hours, but the most important thing is to be capable of running for the whole twenty-four hours – after all, this is not a 100-mile race. Still, now that I'm almost there, I can't stop myself wanting it to be as close to fourteen hours as possible. Something close to fourteen hours would suggest that, as long as I haven't started too quickly, I'm on course for a good performance.

I round the corner again, and Norm and Adrian are nowhere to be seen. *Is 100 miles still some way off, or have I already made it?* I spend the next couple of laps trying to make sense of it all, and then Norm is back. 'You're through a hundred miles, Mike,' he says. The certainty brings an instant relief. On the next lap, Adrian holds out a small piece of paper. I take it as I run past. 'Mike 100 miles 14:17:02.'

I realise that Norm and Adrian had been concerned with getting the time exactly right and recording it in the systems. I carry the piece of paper for a couple more laps, before handing it to Jane with something close to a smile when she comes out to give me a drink.

One hundred miles. The last time I ran that far, I passed towns, farmland and ran along the crowded banks of the Thames. I saw people relaxing in the parks, the last of the day's sunlight reflected on the river, and then wildlife appeared in the beam of my headtorch. And now? I've been running for over fourteen hours and I'm still in the same place.

I feel, though, that I *have* travelled 100 miles. I've seen and experienced many things for the first time. I've both embraced the trip and longed for home. I may only have travelled 400 metres around this track, but I've been on a 100-mile-long journey.

02:28 CONTEXT AND EXPECTATION
101.16 MILES

It is good to have 100 miles behind me, but I made the mistake of focusing for a few minutes on what still lies ahead: well over fifty miles. Worse, I realised that the distance I need to cover is about the same as the Comrades Marathon, which has always been a long race in its own right. This race may not have hills and heat, but I do have the rain and the miles that are already in my legs. It's easier to think vaguely of running until noon than it is to think of a specific distance or to give it a label that makes it too real, or comparable to a past experience.

When I stood at the starting line, my brain had an expectation that I would run for twenty-four hours and cover well over 150 miles. It is that expectation that will make it possible. When I stand at the start of a 56-mile race, that is the expectation in my mind. Everything is geared towards that objective. It's the same thing at the end of a 50-mile training run, when you wonder how you'll be able to go twice as far in your next race. *Because when you start that race, the expectation in your brain is that you'll be running 100 miles, that's how.*

In a 30-mile training run, the last 7 miles may drag. A couple of weeks later, in a 50-mile training run at almost the same pace, those same 7 miles will float anonymously past and everything after 40 miles will probably drag. It's as though the brain works with concepts and percentages, and will start to ask the loudest questions towards the end of whatever it is it has agreed to do.

One of the runs I enjoy least during any campaign is the run the weekend before a major race. Last Saturday, I ran 11 miles at an easy pace. In a normal week, I'll go further than that several times during the week and my long run at the weekend will be further still. But that 11 miles seemed to go on forever. I'd been tapering my training and planned to run hardly at all in the week of the race, so when I started that 11 miles I was thinking that all the months of training were over and that any run I had left would be finished almost as soon as it started. With that in mind, I spent most of it looking at my watch. In comparison, the first 11 miles on this track yesterday were almost unnoticeable because my mind is set on running over 150 miles.

I suppose 50 miles stopped being a very long way the first time I ran 100 miles. And now I'm about to make 100 miles seem a lot less daunting by running much further. When I stood at the start yesterday, the expectation was that I was going to run over 150 miles, and that's what I'm going to do.

02:58 THE RIGHT WORDS CAN MAKE ALL THE DIFFERENCE
104.14 MILES

I am struggling. I've hit a bad patch. The nausea is the main problem because it exacerbates the exhaustion and general sense of physical assault, and also threatens the eating and drinking that is critical to continuing. My crew try desperately to get me to eat and drink something; when I pass him, Norm is shaking bottles of Coke like maracas to make it less fizzy.

I haven't been looking forward to this scheduled feed – as I approach Jane, she holds out a bottle of what looks like Coke mixed with water. I grab it as I pass and continue running until I reach the straight. Then I start my 100-metre walk. I know I'm entitled in my race plan to 200 metres of walking on the hour; I've been sticking to 100, but I decide that now would be a good time to take 200. It may not be on the hour, but I reckon I'm due a break.

I put the bottle to my lips but gag straight away. I try again and manage to force a tiny sip down my throat, followed by another. When I get to the end of the straight, I carry on walking. I manage to force another sip down, so it's been worth the extra break. When I reach the end of the bend and the end of my 200 metres, I don't start to run.

It's fine, I think – *I'll walk the next straight too. I'm sure I read that Marco Consani takes a 400-metre walk every hour, and look what he has achieved. I can use the extra time to sort myself out, to recover a little.*

But when I get to the end of the straight, I carry on walking. I feel terrible – as much as I rationalise what is happening, I know in my heart that this is a crisis. I am now outside of my plan. There's a chance that I will not start to run again, that the part of my brain that wants me to stop will win. Norm and Jane are standing on the track as I walk past. I hand Jane the bottle, avoiding her eye and not looking at Norm. My whole world is crashing in on me.

I'm a few metres past them when I hear Norm: 'This is the part of the race when you need to be running, Mike.' What is it about this simple statement of fact that reminds me of everything I need to do? Is it the bluntness of the reality that if I don't run now, my attempt will be over? Or is it the recognition that I'm not doing what I am supposed to be doing? Who knows what will happen later – maybe I'll be able to walk then, but I *need* to be running now. It's not that I *must*. *Must* is too easy to reject, to challenge. *Don't tell me what I must do – I'll make the decisions.* But do I *need* to run, if I'm going to achieve my dream? Yes.

And so I start to run.

03:10 RACING
105.14 MILES

My bad patch continues – it's a desperate effort to keep running and all I want to do is walk. Paul Maskell comes past me. He's a couple of miles behind me and by unlapping himself, he's closing the gap. If I can just stay behind him, I know it will help me and that he also won't be able to lap me again and catch up. I try to meet his pace but it's no use, and he starts to move away.

'Go with him, Mike,' Norm shouts as we come past on the bend. His voice is loud in the quiet night. Paul is now about 10 metres ahead of me and I make another effort to keep up. This time it works and I maintain the gap. Nothing in the world matters now except staying behind Paul because it means I'm still running. I need to stay there for as long as it takes for this bad patch to pass.

After another lap, I'm still keeping up with him. It's desperately hard but I'm doing it. If I could only get closer then I could get out of the wind and it would be easier to hold on. I make the effort to close the gap – it takes half a lap and then I'm there, right on his back. Running just behind another athlete is noticeably easier in windy conditions – when things are difficult, it can be the difference between keeping going or giving up.

'Stay behind him,' Norm shouts, and I feel slightly embarrassed at the thought that I'm clinging on like a parasite. Normally in a race, I hide from the wind as much as possible – here the atmosphere is so personal that it feels wrong, but right now I don't have a choice. After another couple of laps,

I feel I have to apologise to Paul. 'I'm sorry – I'd normally take a turn with the wind,' I say. I can't make out his reply, but he doesn't sound concerned.

I remember a half marathon some years ago. It was quite windy and I settled in behind another runner to get some shelter, in twelfth position. After a mile or so, I felt a bit guilty and thought I should take a turn in front. I moved onto his shoulder to pass him and he immediately sped up to stop me. I tried again, but the same thing happened – he wasn't going to let me pass. Over the next ten miles, we worked our way through the field. Whenever he started to slow I would move onto his shoulder, but every time he would speed up again. It was a perfect situation: guilt-free drafting, complete with speed control.

By the last mile, there were just two runners ahead of us and we were racing for the final place on the podium. I knew I couldn't trust my sprint, so with half a mile to go I gave it everything I had and overtook before he was able to respond. I heard him breathing behind me for a while and then he was gone. I sprinted into the finish, exhausted but elated. He crossed the line ten seconds later, inconsolable to have missed the podium.

I felt like I'd mugged him at first, but I didn't feel bad for long. I'd tried to take my turn in front and he had not run a good tactical race. Using your head is a big part of racing, although it's not always easy to do the right thing; I once saw a photo of myself racing with a group of about twenty runners behind me. I don't know how long I helped them through the wind, but at the time I had no idea they were there.

I don't want to stay behind Paul for too long. I'm starting

to feel a bit stronger, so as we turn into the wind, I make the effort to pass him. 'I'll go in front for a while,' I say, and it gives me a mental boost. *Maybe Paul and I can take turns for a few hours and help each other around the track*, I think, but then I realise that he's no longer just behind me. I turn around to look and see that he has drifted away from me. For a moment I slow down to give him a chance to catch up, but then I realise that I need to run my own race, as does he. He will have an opportunity to get in behind me if I pass him again, and I hope he does.

03:34 IT'S GOOD TO BE ALONE
107.62 MILES

I love going for a run with my running club on a Sunday morning. My London Heathside clubmates will be starting at 9 a.m. today. Their typical run is around 20 miles long, with a pick up in the pace on the way back. It starts off gently with lots of chatting, and then, as the miles tick by and the pace hots up, the words give way to heavy breathing, the occasional grunt and the sound of feet pounding against concrete. Even when the talking stops, the sense of camaraderie remains.

As much as I enjoy the company, these days I do most long runs on my own. The majority of the group are focused on the marathon, while I have different plans. I prefer to do my very long runs on a Saturday, so I can recover before the working week. Also, in a race I'll be alone and will be constantly aware of my body, and of the signals of tiredness and discomfort. I'll need to pass the time in my own presence, to be patient and to exist without distraction. The only conversation I'll be having will be with myself and the negative thoughts that try to slow me down.

Even when you're running in a team race, you are alone. There's a camaraderie and a shared purpose that can inspire performance, but each of us ultimately face our difficulties in solitude.

Perhaps the best runs to do solo are the longest ones. There we can practise the 'aloneness' of racing, when the sense of achievement and self-belief from the training run is amplified. We learn that we can do it by ourselves. Sometimes it is good to be alone.

03:39 CELEBRATING
108.12 MILES

Not long after I met Jane, she gave me a piece of plain white paper, on which she had drawn the outline of a hand, rough and cartoonish but about life-size. Below it she had written, 'For use on back. Apply regularly.'

We met at the height of the internet boom. At that time, if you were in technology you could be young and hold a position of great responsibility, and that was the case with me. By any normal measure of career progression, I'd achieved a lot in a very short time. However, I derived little pleasure from those achievements. Each felt like the next step on the way to something else, a vague milestone on the frenetic path to some indistinct destination. I never paused to take joy or receive praise. Instead, governed by constant self-assessment, I felt I was basically achieving the minimum required standard. Which was why Jane gave me the drawing of the hand: it was time I started patting myself on the back.

It took a while, but I learned to look for the positives in my achievements rather than focusing on the imperfections. I came to see the value of my work beyond the money and status, such as the opportunity to meet incredible people, and the life experience of doing new or challenging things. To walk into a speech or presentation and think, *Wow, isn't this amazing?* makes for a completely different experience to arriving thinking only about getting it done.

It's easy not to celebrate when life is busy and full of uncertainty. In recent years I've started my own businesses, and while the highs have been very high, the lows have been very low. Good things have happened along the way, and when they do it's too easy to be happy for a moment and then dismiss them as insignificant or say that it's too soon to celebrate. What do we lose by toasting milestones and successes along the way?

Jane is good at insisting that we celebrate our victories, whether they are big or small. Life is often difficult, which is all the more reason to celebrate when things do go our way.

That drawing of the hand now sits in my study. On most days I don't see it, but one day last week I did. I paused for a moment to reflect on how proud I am of the hard work I've put in to prepare for today's race.

In the coming week, Jane and I will no doubt go out to dinner to celebrate our efforts and all that went right, as well as reflect on all that we can learn from what didn't. And every now and then, in the weeks and years that follow, I will sit in my study, fill in my training log and celebrate how I gave it a go.

Those celebrations are one of the greatest rewards of my running: a quiet sense of having done something difficult of which I can be proud. There are no champagne corks or fist pumps, just a momentary glimpse of the serenity which I failed to attain for much of my earlier life.

03:45 VISUALISATION
108.86 MILES

I can hear Tara's voice as if the sound has travelled through the night and entered my ear. It only lasts a second or two, but her positive tone and soft Irish accent are as real in that moment as if she is running next to me.

I've listened to her voice many times as she's led me through visualisations, my eyes closed, oblivious to everything else around me. She has led me down country lanes, across starting lines and finishing straights and around this track.

I have been here before, at this hour. I have seen these scenes as clearly as I could conjure in my imagination, have felt how I feel now and known that it's worth it. I have experienced the difficulty and have been sure of my ability to navigate it. I have known the first light of day, with the joy of the finish still hours away. I know how the story unfolds, so I'm simply putting into effect what I've already seen.

When I talk to Tara, I'm normally sitting in front of the computer at home, with her on the other end of a phone line. She uses photos I send her to construct a picture of the race and talks me through it. 'Over there are the trees, the ones behind the stands. You notice the trees and smile to yourself. You reflect on how good it feels to be here,' Tara says.

The branches hang still and the wind drops, just as it was the last time. I smile to myself – *it is good to be here.* 'You think of what a privilege it is to be part of this,' she says. And I truly do.

PART FIVE

04:00 TO 07:59

04:06 MY HALF-HOUR PLAN
110.85 MILES

It's a relief to finish that feed. Jane handed me the cup of soup and I ran a few steps before starting my 100-metre walk. I tried not to think about it – I just put the rim to my lips and took the liquid into my mouth. I almost swallowed it, but I wasn't quite able to get it down my throat and it sloshed around my mouth. I pressed it through my teeth and finally managed to get it down, followed by another smaller sip. I carried the rest in the cup, looking at it and willing myself to try some more, before throwing it down on the grass as I began to run.

I know it's not enough. I'm aiming for a minimum of 200 calories an hour and what I've just had was almost nothing. But it's the best I can do at the moment, and hopefully it's enough for my blood sugar levels. Maybe it will get me through.

On the very next lap comes the water. My crew know I'm not drinking anywhere near enough and I can tell that they're worried. I dread the drinking almost as much as the food, but I manage to force a little down. It's been plain water for the past few hours, since my declaration: *no more of that salty shit.* A balanced hydration solution with a subtle lemon flavour seems like a nice idea when writing a feeding plan before a race, but in the harsh glare of these stadium floodlights, I'd rather drink my own pee than even look at that crap again.

I have a new half-hour plan: once I'm through the eating and drinking, I'm already seven minutes in. Then I do some laps, knowing that I might soon need to pee, which will give me the chance to stand still for a while. By then, there will be just eleven minutes left; I'm unlikely to be passing my crew exactly on the half-hour, so there's a chance Jane will start the next feed slightly early. This means that there might be just nine minutes of running before she comes out with food and I can have my next 100-metre walk. I'll look out for her a bit earlier than that, which leaves just seven minutes before the end of the half-hour becomes possible. All things considered, it's virtually done already.

04:28 BEING COMFORTABLE
113.09 MILES

I spend a lot of my time in pursuit of comfort – a warm bed, a comfortable sofa and a lazy day resting comfortably at home. Not too hot or too cold, not itchy or sweaty and not too dry. With good food and clothes that feel just right on the skin.

I've worked hard to build a comfortable life for myself. To sleep, travel and simply exist in comfort. Even when camping at the top of a mountain, the coffee in the morning and the wine in the evening are good quality, the treats are abundant and my tent is spacious. My rucksack may be heavy but its straps are comfortable on my shoulders, with much of the weight resting comfortably on my hips.

One night during a camping trip, I wake up in my tent, shivering from the cold ground. My air mattress has a puncture. The tent flaps wildly as the wind roars outside. A pole bends and presses against my shoulder. Too cold to go back to sleep and anxious to check the ropes, I unzip the front of the tent. Despite the wildness of the night, it is the most beautiful sight: the clouds rush past, dropping suddenly to form a mist that plummets into the valley below. The moon appears for a moment and then vanishes into the translucent clouds. My hands ache, rapidly losing their dexterity as I fumble with the ropes.

Drops of ice fall from the tent as I make my way back inside. I try to curl up on top of my empty rucksack but realise I'm not going to get back to sleep – it is too uncomfortable, too cold and too loud.

The incredible sight of those clouds will live with me forever.

And here I am, out on the track – cold, wet, in pain, nauseous and tired. I'm uncomfortable in the extreme. Every step is an achievement. I'm uncomfortable, but I'm definitely alive.

04:33 PAIN
113.59 MILES

I've heard it said many times before: *embrace the pain.* Pain is a strong and emotive word to describe something we experience when bad things happen. Pain is a problem, but what *is* it? The aching in my legs and hips is pain. The sciatic flashes are pain. The jarring in my lower back is pain. The tenderness on the soles of my feet and the blisters under my toenails are pain.

Physical pain is a language and my body has a story to tell, most of which I've heard a hundred times before. The sameness of the plot becomes more boring as the race goes on, so much so that I can eventually barely hear it. There are only so many times the same nerve can complain before I lose interest – what I'm listening for is a new line in the story, or a sudden plot twist.

So I do not embrace, welcome or ignore this kind of pain. Instead, I accept it. It is a fact of running as I do, something I know from experience that I can handle. There is no anticipation, no fear and no dread. It is just something that simply *is.*

Then there are the other things that athletes call pain, sensations for which there is no other adequate word. The anaerobic burn of the sprint, the devouring lactate of the endless hill, the accumulated fatigue of the explosive burst, the exhaustion of endless repetition. It is the sum of sensations, where we take ourselves beyond the realm of comfort. And underpinning it all is the mental strain of coping and finding a way to carry on. I have tried to embrace these things too, but acceptance is more realistic when at the extremes of effort, and even that is difficult at times like these.

Before the race, when I imagine the run, I accept the arrival of those feelings and know that they will be there because I'm doing what I want to do. I don't give it that label, though: pain. Assigning a name to those sensations might add to their power.

How funny. All that preparation and then this – the reality. It is beyond the scope of memory to recall feeling like *this*. After every race I think I can accurately remember the discomfort and prepare myself to face it again. Yet now here I am and it is harder than anything I could ever recreate in my mind. If I could truly recall what this feels like, would I ever have returned?

In this reality, I can try to accept whatever this clusterfuck of difficulty should be called. 'Pain' is a word used for lack of something more adequate, because in many ways this is so much worse. The truth is that if something works for even one moment, it works, and all this can be is a series of moments that can take me to the end.

04:52 A FEAR OF SLEEPLESSNESS
115.58 MILES

Seven or eight hours of sleep is essential for a healthy body and mind, they say, and the fear of not getting it can keep you awake at night.

Jane and I sat with her mother Eve a month ago, as the NHS fought to keep her alive. At 5 a.m., she was stable and we were sent home. We remarked how awake we felt – it seemed that having such a compelling reason to be alert had made staying awake easy. Then we were travelling home in the morning light, the crisis over for a while. 'This is good training for your race,' said Jane.

The thought had been worrying me. I haven't run through an entire night before and some people who have done it say they struggle to stay awake, while others say they hallucinate. I had read that physical exhaustion can dovetail with the need for sleep in the small hours, creating an almost irresistible need to rest. But there I was after a sleepless night filled with focus, tired but fully functional. The physical exertion of the race would make it harder, but I decided not to waste any more time worrying about one sleepless night.

Of the many things I'm coping with now, staying awake is not one of them. There's plenty of caffeine in my system, but the fact that it is late at night doesn't seem relevant – normal time has no meaning here. Whether it's lunchtime, dinnertime or breakfast time, I'm doing the same thing: running around a track, trying to eat and drink every half-hour. The time on this track is not 5.00 a.m. – it's 17 hours.

It is a peaceful time. A number of athletes have been forced to stop by injury, illness or exhaustion, so there are fewer of us running. There's also a sense of quiet beyond the stadium lights, as if everyone in the outside world has fallen silent to watch us. There are few supporters now – it's just the selfless officials and helpers who remain. Is it 5.00 a.m. or 17 hours for them, or are they caught somewhere between the two?

05:04 COMRADES
116.57 MILES

I have another brief conversation with Paul; it's my turn to overtake. I'm glad to gain another lap on him, it is a race after all, and I value the security of a bigger lead. The distance between us has waxed and waned as one or the other has struggled or felt stronger, and it's a relief to be in the ascendancy for a while. At the same time, we've encouraged each other for hours now. If one of us passes the other, there's always a 'well done' or 'keep it up'. I want him to do well – I want to be ahead of him because I'm feeling strong, not because he's struggling.

When this is over, who other than us will understand the experience? What it was like when the rain stopped in the middle of the night, or in the deluge that preceded it. The tiredness, the positive energy from the trackside, the way so many of our fellow runners disappeared without a sound. No wave, no announcement; just gone, one by one, until barely half of us were left.

I was once crewing on a sailing yacht in the English Channel when a huge storm approached. Our racing yacht was built to handle the Southern Ocean, so the decision was taken to head out to sea, even though other ships were rushing for shelter. The storm turned out to be even worse than forecast – before the wind meter on our mast was blown out of service, it had reached hurricane force, and the storm was still building. The crew were working in two shifts and we alternated between hanging onto the deck as the waves came over and lying damp in our bunks listening to the roar as the yacht battled the huge waves. The transition between shifts was the worst – trying to put on or remove boots and heavy weather gear below deck, while feeling at risk of being hurled across the cabin at any moment. It's hard to explain just how bad it was to people who weren't there. By the time the wind started to ease, the crew had gone from near strangers to being connected by the power of this shared experience.

Like any unusual or profound event, it is only those who experienced it who will be able to fully understand. I've since lost contact with the others on the yacht so have no one to talk to about what happened that night, but when this race is over, we will all be participants of a similar shared experience.

It's hard to think of anyone in this race as a competitor – I don't know at what point competitors become comrades, but for me it happened somewhere in the night. It doesn't change my will to win, but it changes what I want for everyone else and how I want them to succeed. The next time I stand at the start I'll feel part of a community, which seventeen hours ago I didn't even know existed.

05:12 THE NEARLY MAN
117.56 MILES

Once a year, there's a 100km race between the British Home Nations, which is the one event at which ultrarunners run on the road for England, Scotland, Wales and Northern Ireland. I dreamed of being selected for England for years, and eventually achieved a time that I thought would give me a realistic chance; when I wasn't selected, I decided that my time had come and gone. I had done my best but had still not been chosen – I just had to accept that I would never wear an international vest.

One night, a couple of weeks after the team selection had been announced, I sat in my study feeling uncharacteristically sorry for myself. The 'nearly man', that's what I was. Close, but not close enough. I'd given it a go and had fallen short.

A few days later, I was on a training run and the phrase came back into my head. Perhaps it was the sunshine, or maybe it was the time that had passed since the announcement, but it sounded like self-indulgent nonsense. Mo Farah, the great Olympian, hasn't piled up the world records, so would he be considered a 'nearly man'? Although Paula Radcliffe has world championships to her name and achieved a marathon world record that's among the greatest sporting achievements of all time, she does not have an Olympic medal – does that make her a 'nearly woman'? In fact, every single person on the planet might be considered a 'nearly person' because whatever they've achieved, there's always the possibility that they might achieve something more.

How easily we get caught up in what we don't manage

to achieve rather than being proud of the effort that got us where we are! There was nothing 'nearly' about my efforts; they were the best I was able to give at the time. I could decide to keep trying or at least to create new goals that would continue to stretch my abilities.

When I got home from my training run, I opened the email I'd received from Walter Hill, the Chief Selector of the England team. In it he'd offered to provide feedback on my rejection. I had nothing to lose by asking – I'd only be a 'nearly man' if I didn't do everything I could.

It took Walter a while to reply. I was starting to think his offer hadn't been serious, but it turned out that the delay was because he was trying to find a world-class coach for me. Walter didn't think I was a 'nearly man', and neither, it turned out, did Norman Wilson. I was a decent runner, and they both knew I would get better with the right help.

The following year, I achieved a higher level of performances and I received an email from Walter Hill confirming my selection for England. The self-belief I gained as a result is part of why I'm here, on this track. And I will continue to try until I know for certain that what I want to achieve is impossible. Wherever I get to, there will be nothing 'nearly' about it. It will simply be the best I could do.

05:24 DETERMINATION
118.81 MILES

Where does determination come from? Having clear goals, pursuing meaningful outcomes and committing completely to the challenge all make a huge difference, but isn't determination also indefinable, the product of that personal blend of DNA and life experience that leads us each to express our will in different ways?

In my first year at university, I joined the skydiving club. I was afraid of heights and had some vague notion of confronting my fear, but I also had an idea that I *had* to do things that were difficult or challenging simply because I could. That it was simply expected of me, by others and by myself. And, of course, I also thought the stories of derring-do might be popular with women – though they weren't.

I only did sixteen jumps but they were over a number of months, during which I lived in almost perpetual fear. If I jumped on a Sunday, I would be ecstatic that evening and Monday might be okay, but for the rest of the week I'd be praying for terrible weather the following weekend, hoping my friend with the car would cancel the next trip or dreaming of catching a bad cold – anything that would mean I couldn't skydive. It just never occurred to me that I had the option to give up.

I must be one of the least suited people ever to have skydived for their university, but I carried on until the National University Skydiving Championship and the chance came to bow out gracefully. At that time, you could jump with round or square parachutes. The square ones allowed plenty of control in the wind and you also could 'flare' before landing, which meant that if you did it right, you could step onto the ground. The round parachutes were hopeless in the wind and you'd always hit the ground like a stone. I chose a round one because jumping with it was cheaper.

Clunky as they were, the only skydivers who would use the round parachutes were the cash-strapped beginners. This meant that team selection for the 'accuracy' competition, which only used round chutes, was easy: anyone willing to do it was in. Our team was hampered by inexperience and also by a jumpmaster who tended to misjudge the wind strength and direction.

To leave the tiny plane, you leaned out of the door, reached for the wing strut with both hands and stretched a foot out onto the wheel below, before stepping onto it. With one foot in the air and your hands still holding onto the wing strut, you looked back through the door at the jumpmaster, who told you when to let go.

I'm still amazed that I was able to step onto the wheel of an aeroplane even once. My determination to do it repeatedly, in the face of complete terror, is something I still don't understand. But if I am doing something, I follow through, no matter what.

Typically, I would let go of the wing and rather than forming the perfect arch position and dropping with control and grace, instead would plummet and tumble through the air, determined to freefall for a while before pulling my ripcord. The realisation that I was going to live was always such a relief – at least until the ground got closer.

The object of the competition was to land as close to the

target – a plastic sheet staked into the ground – as possible. Wherever you landed, you had to remove your parachute and quickly gather it as best you could. The official standing next to the target would then signal that they were starting their stopwatch, and you would run. The clock stopped when you touched the target – if you took longer than two minutes, you would automatically be given two minutes. The team with the lowest total time would win the competition.

On my first jump, having landed just inside the boundary fence, I frantically removed my harness and dragged my chute into an unwieldy bundle. I couldn't see the target, but I could see a distant silhouette in the general direction of who I thought had to be the official. It was too far away to see a signal, so I would just have to assume it had been given. I started to run as fast as possible. It wasn't easy in big boots and with arms full of straps, harnesses and canopy, but I ran and ran, because doing otherwise was unthinkable. Eventually, I could see the target and the official, who looked on as I approached, my lungs bursting. When I reached the bare earth, I sprinted and dived onto the target, landing with a dusty thump. I had done it!

I lay recovering for a few seconds then sat up, chest heaving. I looked over at the official. He stared back. I smiled as I stood. 'What was my time?' He looked at me, dumbstruck. 'Two minutes.'

Of course it was two minutes. It must have been much, much more. I still wonder at what point that official saw a crazed figure sprint out of the haze and inexplicably launch himself into the air. Even now it brings a smile to my face, but on the day, it just didn't occur to me not to try.

Some years later, I competed in an orienteering event organised by my father. I wasn't much of an orienteer, but as my dad had spent many days setting the course, I wanted to support him. I did a few warm-up stretches, cigarette in hand, and then I was off. I rushed around the fields as best I could, and eventually found myself near a river. I followed the bank until the open fields ended and the banks were fenced off on both sides by houses. The only way forward was to continue *in* the river. Steeling myself, I looked at the map again: yes, it was definitely the way to get to the next point. The next half mile took a very long time, as I waded in the water, scrambled over rocks, scaled debris and avoided guard dogs barking from the riverbank. Eventually, I was through; wet, exhausted and covered in scratches, but relieved to have avoided serious injury. I staggered to the point I had been after and then set off for the finish.

When I arrived, it was clear that I was well down the field. My father had a worried look on his face – he had obviously expected me back a lot sooner.

'That river was a killer,' I said.

'River?'

I showed my dad the section on the map and he stared at it in amazement.

'You weren't supposed to go that way,' he said. 'I could have shown that as out of bounds, but it never occurred to me that anyone could think that it was part of the course.'

It turned out that everyone else had just gone around the houses.

Determination isn't always clever or logical. It comes from a place deep inside us, where both great and crazy schemes are conceived, and where a stubborn refusal to accept defeat can lead to life-constraining cul-de-sacs or great success. The trick is to learn to tell the difference.

Whether this race is a grand scheme or fool's errand, I will not be able to complete it without every ounce of determination I can muster. As I think back to the many times in my life I've refused to give up, they fill me with confidence. I wasn't always smart, but I was always brave. And maybe, above all else, determination is a habit.

06:17 FIRST LIGHT
124.03 MILES

I don't see the light arrive – it's simply there, which means that those of us who are left have made it through the night. There's no celebration or joy – there's still too much to be done. For some, it will provide relief from the desperate struggle to stay awake, while it will give others a second wind. For me, the dawn is a milestone I am grateful to tick off.

I realise that for all the hardship I experienced during the night, I found peace there too. The quiet of the track beneath the lights, the anonymity of the passing hours and the stillness as the world around us slept. The sky is brighter now, and I welcome it because it leads us towards the finish. With the melancholy of leaving the quiet behind is the promise of future comfort.

The heavy grey sky is getting lighter. The world is stirring and the hum of traffic rises through the trees like the dawn chorus. I begin to embrace the day but I hope I'll always remember that passing night.

06:26 THE ATHLETE LYING ON THE TRACK
124.77 MILES

A runner has collapsed, and as I come around the bend I see her lying on her back on the finishing straight, the rain pouring down on her. It is a horrible sight. As I get closer, I see that she is surrounded by athletes and helpers. I slow down as I approach but decide not to stop – she needs help from people who have control of their mental faculties and hands.

It is Mari Mauland, the Norwegian runner. The first time we were competing in the same race, we both won it – it was the Thames Path 100, and she flew through the field in the latter stages to finish in fifth place overall. I didn't see her during that race and haven't yet spoken to her today – it feels strange to have so much common experience but not to have exchanged a single word.

As I run, I keep an eye on the people huddled around her. I'm sure that the medics will be there by now. It's a strange thought, but I find myself hoping that it's a sudden injury or hypothermia rather than something more serious; athletes of her calibre don't just hit the floor for no reason.

The incident also pierces through my own focus. The truth is that I could be derailed at any moment – apart from the ever-present risk of injury, there are the wild cards like stomach problems, vomiting and nausea, extreme dehydration, low blood sugar and hypothermia. Many of these things happen during a 24-hour race, but it's just a question of severity and whether they can be put right quickly enough. It's quite common to vomit during a 24-hour race, but the crucial factor is whether the athlete can stop the vomiting and ingest enough liquid and food to make it to the end.

Mari is being brought to her feet – she's wrapped in blankets but conscious. There's no sense of panic, so the situation is obviously under control, which is a relief for all of us. I think of the prayer I said on the starting line: 'Please let everyone get home safely.'

I feel for Mari, for whom over eighteen hours of effort has come to a premature end. Still, while I know she must be distressed right now, I'm sure she'll be back to try again; ultrarunners tend to have incredibly short memories.

06:42 DREAMING
126.26 MILES

If I make it, how will I feel? So much of the joy of the dream is in the imagining. The times when we picture ourselves making it and feel the swell of pride and happiness are almost as profound as the real thing. And sometimes the reality turns out to be less than we'd hoped for. I've imagined the end of this run so many times, but how will I actually feel if I run far enough to know that I've succeeded?

There's that feeling sometimes, after a big event, when the joy fades and all that is left is an emptiness. When you realise your dream, you can be left without one. And what if, when the dream is realised, we're still the same person, with the same challenges and fears?

One of the best moments in my journey to be selected to run for England happened when I was sitting on a bus on a cold night, listening to one of my favourite songs. It was a few days before the 50km race that I knew would decide it, and for the first time I had a real chance of selection and knew exactly what I had to do in that race to make the grade. I saw my reflection in the window and imagined myself at the starting line. For all the nerves, I suddenly knew I was going to do it and felt a surge of excitement and happiness.

That moment is as special to me as the joy of actually making it, and even if I hadn't made it, the moment would have been no less real. The dream is important not just for the motivation it provides, but also for the joy of the imagining.

06:55 CONTROLLING THE WEATHER
127.51 MILES

In the weeks before the race, I thought a lot about the weather. The forecast looked good until last weekend, when wind and rain suddenly seemed likely. Unhappy with that prediction, I scoured numerous websites for a more acceptable forecast. One website was a lot more optimistic than the others: the future wasn't exactly *bright*, but it was definitely a lot less grim. However, a couple of days later, that website was also predicting wind and rain.

Now that I knew what to expect, I should have been able to get on with my other preparations and forget about the weather; instead, I continued to check hourly forecasts, to see how much of the time I might be wearing my rain jacket. Quite a lot of the time, all the websites and apps said.

But predicted rain is so often no more than a heavy cloud and a few drops. How bad could it be? Well, quite bad as it turns out. After a week of worrying that the weather would be as bad as predicted, I can confirm that it is much, much worse. And despite all my time spent planning, the weather has proven extremely difficult to control.

07:12 GOING IN AN ANIMAL
129.00 MILES

When I was in my twenties, my body was just the thing that carried me to work, a necessary inconvenience that delivered me to meetings before carrying me back home. Once there, it pointed my heavy eyes towards the TV as I tried to relax with alcohol and nicotine. Shrouded in clothing and almost grey with neglect, my body was unnoticed and unloved.

An occasional visit to the gym would awaken me to my body's potential. The pumped feeling in the muscles made me feel instantly fitter, and for a few days I would walk around aware of my shoulders, my arms and my posture. I'd smoke a bit less, eat a salad and resolve to look after myself. But I'd always forget.

One apparently unremarkable moment stands out for me: I was driving past a runner in the sunshine at a time in my life when I was living on pizza and toasted cheese sandwiches. I was hungover and smoking a cigarette. I looked at him and felt a yearning to be that healthy person running in the sunshine rather than the physical delinquent driving past him.

In my late teens, my friend Eddie and I started to take training in the gym very seriously. Our focus was on building muscle; fitness was irrelevant – it was all about looking strong and attractive. We didn't judge our progress by a match won or a time achieved, but by a favourable reflection in the mirror or a compliment from a friend at the gym. One day, I was keen for the feeling of aerobic exercise and got on the treadmill to run. After a few minutes, a couple of friends came up to me, looking concerned. 'You do know you'll lose weight if you run?' they asked. To them, running was an act of self-harm: losing size for no discernible gain. In fact, the thought *had* occurred to me and five minutes later I was off the treadmill, determined not to get back on it anytime soon.

When I started running regularly many years later, it was the first time in my life that my body shape was about utility rather than appearance. As I increased the intensity of my training, I started to lose much of the hard-earned muscle in my shoulders and biceps, and my waist shrunk. I didn't just lose a bit of weight – my whole body shape changed.

We tend to be careful about telling people that they're overweight, but we're less hesitant when it comes to thinness. At first, having people tell me I was really skinny didn't feel great, as a man who'd spent many years trying to be bigger. But then I stopped caring, mainly because I felt so good. And as my running became more important to me, I began to see my leanness as a massive positive. Bigger biceps might be nice, but very few runners wish they were heavier when the starting pistol goes off at the start of a race. Being healthy and lithe would be just fine.

My friend Rob, who is part of my crew today, and I began talking about how to get into shape for a race; about cutting out wine and chocolate, maximising training and taking physical and mental preparation to the next level. Our aim was to become primed for effort, endurance and toughness. I always smile when I think of how he describes this objective, but it also conjures up images that give me confidence. The plan is not simply to be fit, strong, lean or tough; it is to be something primal and fit for purpose. When you're entering an important race, you should be *going in an animal.*

07:45 KINDNESS
132.23 MILES

A woman stands alone in the rain, playing an instrument that looks like a flute. She's on the inside of the track at the start of the bend. The sound doesn't travel far in the wind, but it follows me down the straight and each time I approach, I'm surprised to see her there.

I don't recognise the song she's playing and there's no beat to drive me on. What helps me, though, is that she cares enough to be here, standing in the cold and wet. What, other than kindness, would make her play her music in such a place at such a moment?

There is so much kindness in the world when we look for it. When I was on crutches after my ankle operation, I was struck by how many people wanted to help me as I tried to get around London. Then there are the moments of kindness that touch us in unusual or profound ways.

One such instance happened when I was working as a construction labourer while travelling around the world. One day, I was walking across the creaking tiles of the roof of an enormous mansion when it collapsed beneath my feet. I fell three or four metres, landing on my back on a ceiling beam. Lucky not to have broken any bones, I was covered in bruises and cuts. Incredibly, as I tried to climb down into the kitchen, the primary concern of the owner seemed to be that I didn't bleed inside the house. My bosses didn't want to take me to a doctor because I had no work permit, so I was cleaned up by one of their girlfriends and dropped off at my hostel.

At the hostel we slept in rooms with around six bunks in each.

It was a very sociable place, with young travellers constantly arriving from all over the world, and it was small enough that when something like my accident happened, the word spread quite easily. That evening I sat quietly on the open, flat roof, very sore, drinking beer and listening to people's conversations. Most of the men didn't wear shirts as it was so hot, so my injuries were there for all to see. I was feeling sorry for myself and very alone.

Eventually, I limped downstairs to try and get some sleep, past the open door of another room. I heard someone call out to get my attention from a bottom bunk; it was a Dutch woman, one of a group who had arrived earlier that day. Her friends were also in the room.

'Hey,' she said softly. I walked towards her, unsure what she wanted. 'I heard you got hurt,' she said. 'Come and sit down here.'

As I approached, she sat up and held out her arms. I sat down shyly and she put her arms around me, unphased by my injuries, and held me quietly. In that moment, I didn't have to be tough and I was no longer alone. All the shock came out and I began to cry, as she stroked my hair and told me that everything was going to be all right. After a while I stood up; I can't remember if I thanked her, but my eyes would have said more than any words could. And then I left the room.

She must have left early the next morning, because I never saw her again and I never learned her name. Even now I feel touched by her kindness, and I still can't tell the story without my throat tightening and tears coming to my eyes. I get taken back there every time; not to the trauma and the loneliness, but to the relief and the kindness.

I hope she is happy, wherever she is.

07:54 SECOND WIND
132.97 MILES

All of a sudden, someone appears on my shoulder and moves past me. I've been overtaken a few times during the race, but nothing like this. The speed of it, so outside of the natural rhythm of the race, is almost shocking. I didn't hear them coming – I've been focusing on the flapping of my hood, the patter of the raindrops and the incessant gusts of wind, but this runner is just suddenly there.

My immediate response is to be embarrassed that I wasn't able to give way on the inside lane – I've been given the shortest line on so many occasions that to not do the same feels unforgivable. Perhaps I'm overreacting as a result of the stress that my body and mind are under, but I'm mortified.

Then it sinks in that one of the other runners is also moving very quickly and that this is a race. Working out who is difficult, but I know it isn't Paul – and he's closest to me in terms of distance. Surely no one else would be able to close the gap in the remaining time, or have I horribly misunderstood the situation? Is someone going to come flying through and win at an incredible pace?

The other problem is the reduced hearing and peripheral vision that I have as a result of my hood. To spot the quicker runner approaching requires an almost constant twisting around, which uses energy and affects my rhythm. It explains why some people are running in the second lane, in order that there's always space for other runners to pass on the inside. Others have given up trying to move aside, no longer able to endure the cost in energy and rhythm of anything other than the simplest route to the finish.

I read the board at the starting line as I pass to remind myself of the latest distances. Paul is still a couple of miles behind me, and the next runner is what feels like an insurmountable way further back. It's not long before he's at my shoulder again. The fog has cleared enough from my brain to know that in order for my lead to be threatened, he would need to be overtaking me with incredible regularity.

This time, I'm able to catch a glance at the side of his face. I think it's David Bone, and he seems to be moving faster than anyone since the beginning of the race. Either that or I'm moving a lot slower, or both. What second wind has gifted him such strength at this stage, and will he be able to keep it going?

It might seem counter-intuitive, but I sometimes feel better after three or four hours of running than I do after one. Yes, there's a general stiffness and ache, but there's also a flow, a mental acceptance of the purpose of the movement. If you feel bad, it's good to know that you may feel better later; having a bad first hour or two doesn't necessarily mean a bad run.

The same can apply to any distance – a new runner looking to cover 5km should remember that they may feel better after four kilometres than they do after two. At the 24-Hour European Championships in 2018, Great Britain's James Stewart ran faster in the last hour than he had at any point during the previous twenty-three, an incredible achievement that even he may have been surprised by. However hard everything feels now, I remind myself that the runner flying around the track in the final hour could be me.

PART SIX

08:00 TO 12:00

08:15 BOREDOM
134.96 MILES

'Won't it be boring?' is one of the most common questions people ask about running in a race like this. To which the answer is as follows:

'If you were to do something once or twice a year and most of the time you were in pain and feeling ill was guaranteed. If it made you tired to the point of exhaustion, hour upon hour. If it involved making decisions almost constantly, to avoid obstacles in your path. If its highs and lows were so intense that they were capable of redefining your sense of self and if the thing had the potential to completely transform what you thought was possible. If it challenged you mentally, physically and emotionally to the very core of your being. Would it be boring?'

08:52 TRYING HARD
138.19 MILES

The best race I've ever run was the British 100km Championships. I finished in bronze medal position wearing an England vest. Just to be in that race was a dream, but to get a national championship podium finish, alongside athletes of the class of Robert Turner and Anthony Clark, was beyond belief. If I do nothing else ever again, I'll always have that.

It wasn't easy. In the last ten miles, on top of the usual exhaustion and pain, something happened. I can only describe it as my legs and brain being out of sync. What is it when your brain thinks your legs are ahead of where they really are and you lose the ability to match the actual movement of your muscles with the sensations of movement? At times, I felt like my physical self was running to catch up with where my brain thought I'd got to. It felt like I was getting two versions of reality: one from my brain and one from my body.

With a mile to go, I desperately turned to look for Scotland's David McLure, who I knew was closing in on me, and for a few frightening moments I felt like I had no real control of my movements, as if my brain couldn't handle the change in perspective. When I arrived at the finish, the pressure in my head was so severe that I felt like I was clinging on to consciousness. As I listened to the applause and the words of the announcer, I had to hang onto a fence to stay upright.

I don't know what happened that day – at points my physical and mental realities were in different places, but within a minute after the race, I felt normal. Apparently, during those final ten miles I did look normal, even though I felt like my legs were visibly jerking erratically with each stride.

It was a great performance – not because of those issues, but because I used every fragment of available mental and physical resource and arrived at the finish line with nothing left to give. I never again want to feel whatever that was, but I don't fear it because I doubt it will ever happen again. Sometimes, at the extremes of performance, weird stuff happens. On one occasion at the Berlin Marathon, I lost the ability to hold my head up, so I ran the last 5km mostly staring upwards. I could only look forward by peering out the bottom of my eyes. It wasn't pretty, but I managed to run a personal best, and it never happened again.

One of my talents is the ability to try hard at whatever I do. In life, trying hard fills a lot of gaps in other talents. At the end of my first year of school, I won the prize for *tenacity*. I had no idea what that was – I just knew I had won a prize and that all was right with the world.

'It means you try hard,' my mother explained.

As I got older and more cynical, tenacity began to sound more like: *didn't make the grade but should be encouraged.* But right now, tenacity sounds like a prize worth winning.

Like any positive attribute, trying hard has its shadow – not knowing when it's time to give up, and the potential for burnout – but with self-awareness, effort can be directed in the right places.

I've also learned that however hard I try, there will always be someone who tries harder. There is a long, steep hill at the Comrades Marathon called Polly Shortts which comes after 50 miles on the run to the city of Pietermaritzburg. Everyone struggles with the gradient and the heat, and all but a few walk at some point. I was once doing exactly that, when another runner came past me very slowly. He was barely running, but he exuded a level of effort I had never seen before. The contortions on his face, the desperate breathing, the incredible strain in his shoulders and arms, and an absurd lean to one side were the embodiment of effort and agony. I believe his dream was to run all the way up Polly Shortts and that on that day he would have died rather than walk. I overtook him each time I managed to run for a bit, but each time I walked he came past me again. He got to the top without walking, probably one of a dozen out of 16,000 who did. He tried hard and he made it, and no one can ever take the day he ran the whole way up Polly Shortts away from him.

09:02 SEEING THE RAIN
138.94 MILES

I grab the soup from Jane, trying not to crush the paper cup. I run a few more steps and the liquid sloshes onto my hand. I start to walk, putting the cup to my mouth. My movement isn't smooth and the soup spills onto my chin. I force my lips open and manage to swallow a small amount before I gag. As I arrive on the straight, I try again and force a bit more down my throat. The brief warmth of it inside my chest is wonderful, but it can't stop me shivering.

Suddenly there's someone walking beside me, asking how I am. I know his face but it takes my brain a couple of seconds to work out that it's Dan Lawson, winner of many international trail races, a former European 24-Hour Champion and one of the best runners Britain has ever produced.

Dan tells me that he is about to go for a training run in the park but the rain's so bad he's having second thoughts. I look around, having barely even glanced beyond the track for the past couple of hours. Puddles have turned into streams, raindrops are bouncing off everything and the outside world is indistinct behind a screen of water.

'It's wet,' I confirm, struggling to talk through the shivering.

'Looks like we'll be seeing you at the world championships next year, if you carry on like this,' Dan says.

I try to force some more soup down as his words sink in: *he's right, and he should know.*

I'm halfway down the straight now. The shivering is becoming unmanageable.

'I'm sorry,' I say. 'I have to run. I'm so cold.'

I throw the cup onto the grass inside the track and start to run. Dan disappears, like a vision that was never truly there. Only the implications of what he had to say remain; he believes I'm going to do it. And so do I.

09:35 STEPPING BACK
141.92 MILES

For the first five years of my life, my family lived in a third-storey flat, and I remember being convinced that the building was falling down. I would lie in bed terrified that our home was about to collapse onto the ground below. One night after I cried out, my father took me out of bed and we walked out of the flat, along the corridor, down the stairs and onto the grass below. There we stood in the evening light, my hand in his, looking up at the block of flats. It was as solid and immovable as ever. Then we walked back up the stairs and along the corridor, and I was soon back in bed. I never again thought the building was collapsing.

I imagine my father in his lounge, thousands of miles away, watching as my lap times appear in the live results on his screen. For a moment I am there with him, looking at the total miles I have run, and I know that no single moment of doubt or difficulty will easily destroy what is now possible.

09:43 MAY AS WELL SMILE
142.92 MILES

There are a few people on the track who have a natural and infectious inclination to smile. I almost run into one of them; I'm about to pass her when she steps out, trying to give me the shorter inside line.

'Sorry!' she says, laughing beneath her rain hood.

We've been running for over twenty hours, it's pouring with rain and we're digging deep into reserves we didn't know we possessed as we keep our exhausted bodies moving forward. *Is this really the time to be laughing?* Of course it is. Susie Chan is famous for smiling her way through ultra-distance events in deserts, jungles and now on athletics tracks. She isn't cruising around, either – she's in considerable pain, but she's still somehow able to smile.

I've tried it myself. In my only international appearance for England earlier in the year, I decided to make the effort to smile whenever I took a drink or gel from Jane, to show her I was okay and to convince my brain that everything was going well. It worked for three hours, until the reality of racing overwhelmed anything other than my most basic instincts.

Andy, my mental performance coach, has told me that just making the shape of a smile with your mouth can send positive signals to the brain. I sometimes try it during difficult training sessions on the treadmill and it usually works for a moment or two, even if only due to the distraction.

Are we born with the ability to laugh and smile in stressful times or can we cultivate it? If the latter, it is not just a talent but a skill to be gained and mastered. And unlike some skills, smiling has the added benefit of positively affecting others. I will owe at least a few metres of my distance today to almost bumping into Susie Chan.

09:52 TIME
143.66 MILES

For a long time in this race, I was largely able to ignore the clock. It told me where I was within my thirty-minute cycle between feeds, but otherwise I was so far away from the end of the race that the time seemed irrelevant. Now, though, I can't keep my eyes off it. I know that logically it will only move on by two or three minutes with each lap, so what's the point in looking?

Keep your eyes down and don't look.

Two minutes and some seconds gone. How many more laps to the end of my thirty-minute horizon? That's the worst thing: starting to calculate the number of laps before the next walk break and ticking them off one by one – the minutes and laps have to be anonymous, or each will last forever.

I think back to those first hours on this track when time rushed by; then it was a thing of minutes and hours, whereas now it is a thing of seconds and minutes. Soon my world will be made up of moments and seconds – unless I'm able to stop looking at that clock.

Don't look. Lose yourself in time.

About two and a half minutes gone. I know better than to wish away even one day of precious life, but surely a few hours would be okay? To sacrifice this morning and for it to be afternoon already, with the race done. To be lying on the couch at home, revelling in the memory of the race.

Revelling in the memory of *what* though – once it's gone, what will be left? A result on a sheet of paper, or the knowledge of having achieved something I don't fully recall?

Surely I should think of the time to go as a blessing? After all, the more time I have left, the further I can run, and what is this all for if not to run as far as possible?

What does it matter? I have no choice now any more than I do when I want a moment to last forever. Whether it is fast or slow, time seems to have its own tempo, which is always the opposite of what we want.

10:27 HOPE
146.65 MILES

Another lap. I don't know if it's the lack of food, the cold or the tiredness, but it's becoming harder to think. Why am I here? What is this all for? And does any of it matter?

The rain continues to fall, and as I turn onto the straight a gust of wind smashes into me, almost stopping me completely. I stagger slightly and am pushed across the lane by another gust. My jacket fills up with air like a parachute, slowing me down. I try to pull the hood tight around my face, but the wind finds gaps and inflates my sleeves like balloons.

At last I reach the bend and then the wind seems to come from everywhere at once, lashing rain across my face and whipping into my bare legs. I complete the turn and am shoved forward. It should feel better than it does: my soaking jacket presses into my back and the uneven gusts put me off my stride.

My purpose feels vague; there's only the cold and the wet and the need to carry on. I start to pee. It is a deliberate decision – at least I think it is. The warmth is glorious. I look down at my legs as I run; the stream is barely discernible in the downpour. Should I stop it? I'm nearing the bend where there are plenty of crew, huddled in tents. The warm flow stops. I look down at my legs again, but they've been cleaned by the rain. I feel self-conscious for a moment and then smile as the wind hits me once again.

My shivering has a tune, I realise. *Sha, sha, sha.* Are those words or just sounds? Am I moving in time to them? *Sha, sha, sha.* I don't have to make that sound, but I do as I exhale because I want to. I decide to stop it. Then, when it comes back with my next breath, I know that I could choose to stop it again if I wanted to.

The wind is blowing right into my face and it's making me feel like I'm running on the spot. I think about how sick I feel. Should I vomit? Would it help? But that doesn't seem to matter – I'm just a boat caught in a storm, being pushed this way and that, and will end up finishing somewhere once the wind and rain have passed. It is not up to me.

It must be the lack of sugar that's causing this blurry mind. Jane will be there soon and I'll be able to drink some soup and clear my thoughts. Until then, I'll keep on making these steps through the shivering and the pain. Each step is taking me closer to the end. And where there's progress, there's hope.

10:59 THIS SINGLE HOUR
149.63 MILES

Paul is running faster than me. He overtook me not long ago, and at the pace he was going, I know it won't be long before he's here again. The negative voice in my head is loud: *winning doesn't matter, you've done enough already. You can walk if you want to.* But that's a lie. I've been here before. And I think back to my race notes: 'When you are tired, you might try to convince yourself that racing for a specific distance or place doesn't matter, but it does.' The voice tries again, but I know whether I'll be feeling regret or joy at the end of the race will depend on my willingness right now to keep running.

The race board only updates every hour. I don't trust my brain to compute anything, but I need to know exactly how many laps Paul is behind me. Then I'll only need to remember one number and to subtract one from it each time he comes past. If I ensure it is above zero at the end, I'll have won.

Then Rob is on the track, holding out a bottle of Coke. I start to walk as I take it from him and in a few steps I try to explain what I need to know. The words don't come out easily but I think he understands what I'm asking. I walk a little further and start to run again. It might be the sugar in the drink or maybe it's the importance of the situation, but my head feels a little clearer. *It all comes down to this last hour.*

What I do in this hour will define me. When everything was possible, did I run or did I walk? Did I win or did I surrender my lead? Did I go far enough to run for Great Britain? Did I fight with everything I had for what I wanted or did I fall short? How will I feel for the rest of my life about what happens in this single hour?

There's no sign of Rob as I'm running the next lap, but then he appears by the starting line, near the timing system. 'Eight,' he says. 'Paul is eight laps behind.' I don't know if that's good or bad. It sounds like enough, but if I start to walk or have any major problems, Paul will close me down in no time. And now he's on my shoulder again. We each manage a word of encouragement to the other as he passes.

Eight minus one is seven. Seven laps. Already he has pulled away by ten, twenty, thirty metres and I can't follow. This is going to be a fight to the very end.

11:03 THE GIFT OF PERSPECTIVE
149.88 MILES

When I was thirty-five, I was sent for X-rays to investigate a back problem. My doctor called to say that I would need to go for some scans and blood tests, as the X-rays had shown up something that required further investigation. A few days later, I had MRI and CT scans. A few days after that, I found myself walking into an oncology outpatient ward. My doctor pointed to a room and said, 'That's where you'll stay after chemo, if you need to.'

I stood with the oncologist, looking at images of what he said was a lymphoma near my spine. The problem, he said, was how to get at it without causing damage to the spinal cord or major arteries. Over the next week there were more blood tests, scans and examinations. Jane and I were afraid, but we were closer than ever as we tried to get our heads around this new reality. Though we were in a daze, we continued to do normal things and decided not to tell anyone until we had a full prognosis.

One day, the oncologist told me one of his colleagues thought she could get a better look using ultrasound, and a few hours later she was pressing the scanner into my belly. 'I don't think there's anything there,' she said, smiling.

It was an anomaly: some combination of flesh or water presenting as something in the scans. I would need to come back a few times to make sure the image hadn't changed shape or size, but it was highly likely that everything was okay. The oncologist apologised for putting me through such a stressful experience, but I was too busy thanking him to complain.

I was recently seeing my GP, Ann – the doctor who walked with me into the oncology outpatient ward. She is a real intellect and possesses a vivacious and engaged interest in everything. We were talking about some minor health issue I was dealing with when she said with a chuckle, 'But I know that won't bother you after we scared the hell out of you with the lymphoma thing. Nothing like a bit of perspective.'

The perspective I gained from the cancer scare was nothing compared to someone who has dealt with actual illness, but in those couple of intense weeks, I certainly saw things differently. The first thing I did on that last day, before leaving the hospital, was write down the things that I had learned. I keep the notebook in my desk. The hasty scrawl reveals a fear that at any moment the learning would fade, as it sunk in that I was fine and that normal life could resume.

I wrote how over the past two weeks the colours had seemed so bright. How I realised that the things that gave my life meaning were all very simple. How you can see goodness in everything when you look for it. How there is very little that is truly worth fretting about. And how the pursuit of happiness is meaningless without kindness.

I like to think that I still carry that perspective with me, but in truth it is all too easy to be consumed by petty concerns, to see the bad in everything, or to fail to notice the beauty in life. Right now, though, there is a certain clarity. I think of Eve, so ill but still eager to laugh. I remember spending the last few hours of my 100-mile race knowing that everything would be all right if I could get to the finish to see Jane. I think of my friends and family supporting me, both at the side of the track and far away. I dream of being at rest, of the warm feeling of my favourite fleece top and of a picnic in our local woods. And for a moment, instead of the rain, I see the light and how it shimmers in the sky, and it is beautiful.

11:28 BACK TO THE BEGINNING
152.11 MILES

Norm is standing on the track just past the starting line. There are other people there too, but I don't see their faces. 'One lap to 245 kilometres,' he shouts. 'One lap.'

Before the race that was the number we felt we needed as a minimum; 245km, just over 152 miles. It's well past the GB qualifying standard, but with so many others vying for places, under 245km and selection will be unlikely. Every step beyond 245km will increase my chances of making the team.

On the far side of the track, I run past my crew. I'm half expecting to eat something but there's no one there with a bottle or cup. Jane is at the table getting something ready, so it will be there the next time I pass. Suddenly, I feel like these past 245km were not the race at all; they were what I needed to do to get to the start. The race begins now, and these are the yards that will count.

Soon I'm running down the straight, into the wind. This time Norm is quite animated. '245 kilometres, Mike,' he shouts as I approach. There's only a very slight smile on his face – he knows there's still a lot to do. I hold out my hand and give him a high five as I pass. The gesture brings me out of myself; moments ago I hardly felt capable of lifting a hand to wave.

When I get back to my crew, Jane is holding out some soup. I can barely believe it, but this is the last feed, and my next half-hour horizon will be the last. I don't know how Jane feels, whether she is thinking the same thing. 'It's 245 kilometres,' I say. She says something – I can tell from her tone that it's positive, but the exact words don't make it through my hood as I run on.

At the start of the straight I begin my walk and force down some of the soup. Paul comes past, running well, reducing my six-lap lead by one. *Six minus one is five.* Is it possible for him to catch up with me in half an hour? If I do not walk, can he run fast enough? What kind of pace would he need? I try to do the maths but it's impossible. I throw the cup to the ground inside the track and start to run.

11:35 THE GATHERING CROWDS
152.61 MILES

The crowds grow louder. This end of the track is like a tunnel of sound; it feels like hundreds of voices, though I know it is far fewer than that. After the silence of the night it's as if we've been transported to the streets of London during the marathon.

'It's number forty-six again! Amazing!' a woman calls out each time I pass. I listen for her each time and wonder who she has come to support. I can't see her – that would require me to turn and look as I pass, which feels impossible. I see only a tunnel a few lanes wide with a blurred wall at its edge. I try to wave a thank you, but my hand and arm barely move.

It feels like I'm running at an amazing speed, flashing past the crowd, though I know that's not the case. Who are these people who have come to stand in the rain and watch the culmination of an insane act of physical defiance, and how does it feel to watch this human drama unfold? It feels so fast from here, but for them the scene is surely less frantic as we hobble past one by one, racing in slow motion.

I feel grateful to every one of them, and for a moment I think my eyes are filling up. They are gathering because it is almost over. I am nearly at the end.

11:50 WITHIN REACH
154.00 MILES

Shankara, the Race Director, is holding out some markers as I pass. My number will be written on one of them. It seems impossible, but we've finally reached that time. Each athlete, or a helper – usually a family member or supporter – will carry their marker. When the final hooter sounds, we will stop and mark our finishing point on the track, so the partial lap we completed can be measured and added to our distance.

I'm suddenly certain that I will run to the very end. It is the first time in this entire race that I've known this for sure. I try to enjoy this final run-in, but each moment passes so slowly that being so close is like a new kind of agony. *Please just let it be over.*

I think of Eve at the hospice with Anni updating her as I complete these final laps. I think of my parents and my sister Anne, watching the live results on computer screens so far away, and I know that they will be proud. And most of all, I long for Jane and an end to this time that stands between us.

11:58 THE END
154.60 MILES

As I reach the starting line, Jane is there. I've dreamed of this moment for many hours and have imagined it for many months. She'll run the last lap, or however far we get before the hooter sounds, with me. I take her hand and feel an immense surge of happiness. Her support over the years has been boundless and unconditional. We're a team and what we achieve, we achieve together.

As we run around the first bend, I begin to laugh. It feels almost surreal to have her with me on the track. My mind is clearing – perhaps as a result of the adrenaline. 'Do you have the marker?' I ask her.

'Norm has it.'

We are now on the far straight and Norm is running next to us.

'Run!' he shouts, his voice stern. 'It's a race!'

Perhaps in his many years of coaching, he's seen too many races lost on the final lunge for the line and dreams shattered by a few metres surrendered. The race doesn't end until the final gun.

Jane and I both smile and she lets go of my hand so I can move more freely. We round the far bend and I long for the sound of the horn. I don't care about distance or winning anymore – the sound of the horn is all that matters.

And then it comes: a high-pitched blast that's the most wonderful thing I've ever heard. I stop running and Norm places my marker on the ground. There will be no more miles. It is over.

Jane is in my arms now and we are laughing. Tears roll down my cheeks. The relief is infinite. 'You did it,' she says, her voice faltering.

Then I turn to Norm. I have so much to thank him for. He offers a hand, which I ignore, and we hug.

I can't believe it's over. And then Rob, Helen and Toby are with me too, and we're all hugging. My gratitude to them is absolute.

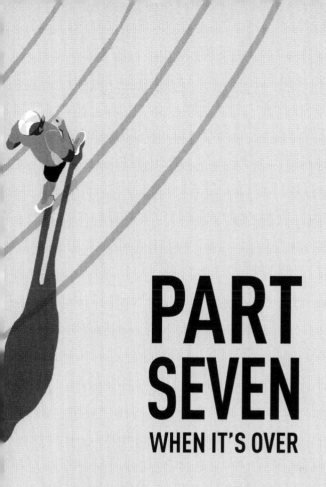

PART
SEVEN
WHEN IT'S OVER

12:04 THE BRAIN DECIDES

It's amazing how the legs stop working the moment I reach the end. During a race, we can walk or stop for a moment, and although we might be stiff and sore, we can start running again. But when we cross the line and stop, our legs seize up completely and running becomes impossible.

We've convinced our minds that the body is capable of reaching the end for many hours. We have negotiated and harangued. Deals have been done. *Get me to the next lap and then we'll see.* And now we are there, at the end. Our brain finally wins: the race is over, and we won't run another step.

As we walk towards the warmth of the changing rooms, I lean on Jane for balance. I can barely bend my legs and the calf that forced me to stop many hours ago has completely seized up. What will happen when we get to the changing rooms? Only my brain can decide.

12:05 SPORTSMANSHIP

People I've never spoken to before, beyond a tired 'thank you' or half-wave during the race, are congratulating me. The generosity of their words stuns me. One of them is David Shaw. It has not been a good race for him by his high standards, and he left the track at some point during the night. This is not an event that you can have another go at next week – it might be another year before he's able to try again. His face tells a story of torment and of the months of analysis that await him. But despite his own disappointment, he's here to congratulate those who made it to the end and he tells me how much he enjoyed watching me run.

I think of what I'd be doing in his situation – would I still be here, so many hours later? Would I have the courage to show my support for the other athletes, or would I be consumed by my own difficulties? In this moment, David's spirit of sportsmanship overrides everything else.

12:07 GREATNESS AND HUMILITY

Marco Consani has won this race before, as well as many others, including the prestigious Lakeland 100. He has represented Great Britain numerous times in 24-hour running and is the standout elite athlete at this event.

He's had injury problems this year and today just wasn't his day – despite fighting on for many hours, he eventually dropped out. Many would have headed home at this point, unable to watch others do well in a race they might have won. Others might have stayed to make it known that they've been injured and expected nothing from today. Marco is here to offer congratulations and to be part of our community, not to make excuses.

Marco's chance to earn selection to the GB team is over for this year – the time between now and December is too short for him to try again. Instead, he's watched as Paul and I made the GB standard. He has been encouraging to me throughout the race and is gracious in his congratulations.

I think about the people who carry a label of rank or achievement – the sportspeople, the politicians and the business leaders – and about how some of them lack the humility to act with honesty and grace when they've fallen short, but who instead blame others and deflect responsibility from themselves. Who big themselves up by putting others down. Who hide self-doubt behind a façade of importance. Who substitute leadership and class with arrogance and rudeness. And who lose touch with empathy and kindness in their descent to supposed greatness.

When I look at the people here, I wonder whether humility

is easier in a sport where complete physical and mental breakdown is a constant possibility. Everyone here has been the person who didn't make it. In this sport, fame is limited to a group of peers, and the winnings often amount to a box of energy bars or a voucher for some new running shoes. Perhaps the physical and mental trials of the sport remind us of our inherent humanity. Whatever the reason, as I watch Marco walk away, I'm struck by his dignity and self-awareness, and how he expects nothing other than to be treated just like everyone else.

12:09 NATURE HAS A SENSE OF HUMOUR

It started raining yesterday as we were preparing for the start of the race. There was a period during the night when it stopped but then, as if to make up for the oversight, the morning light signalled the start of an even greater deluge. Now that the race is over, the rain has stopped again, and the sun is laughing at us from behind the thinning clouds.

12:15 GETTING DECENT

I've started to shake. I was shivering a lot for the last five hours of the race, but now that I've made it to the changing rooms and taken off the jacket that Jane threw over me at the finish, it's got even worse. I don't really care because the race is over, but I'm unable to grab anything and I need help undressing. My fingers are also frozen and stiff. My hands have become swollen with fluid that was retained as my system prioritised more essential functions. My knuckles are visible beneath the skin but make no impression on the surface of my hands.

Rob and Toby have to help me get undressed. I feel a bit foolish, as most of the runners around me don't need help, but my hands aren't really working and the shaking is making everything difficult. I don't care though – I'm just so relieved and happy. I also have the assistance of a medic who gives me something to drink – I have no idea what it is, but I manage to get some of it down.

As my socks come off, I look at my feet. It had felt for many hours like the sole of my right foot had split but it's just swollen, with a bit of skin separation from the damp. I realise that I've run 250km without once changing my shoes or retying a shoelace.

There's a big bruise on the side of my foot where the blood has been collecting from my calf injury for the past fourteen hours. The calf itself is swollen and bruised. How on earth have I run for fourteen hours with a calf strain? Would that have been possible had I stopped and seen what I'm seeing now?

Eventually I'm back from the shower, and my friends

help me get dressed. The dry warmth of the fresh clothes is wonderful beyond description. I quickly start to warm up and regain my independence.

12:52 PRIZES

The prize-giving is on the terrace looking out towards the track. It is strange to see it from this angle, both foreign and familiar. There are not that many chairs but I have taken one of them without a moment's hesitation, though I would normally have been more polite. I don't think anyone has left the grounds: runners, supporters, organisers and crew are all here.

Shankara Smith holds the microphone. I feel self-conscious and proud as I hear her words: 'First, in 154 miles 790 yards, or 249.11 kilometres, was Michael Stocks from London Heathside.'

Many years ago, I ran a 10km race where the over-fifty category was won by someone who ran it in just over thirty-two minutes. When it was announced, there was a collective murmur of surprise. I hear a similar sound as Shankara reads out my distance – in some ways I can't believe it myself. We all came to this race knowing that it would be won with this kind of distance, yet to hear it announced feels different to reading a result on a website. How is it possible to have run so far? By keeping going at a decent pace for a long time, I know, but it still surprises me. I limp over and gratefully take the trophies for first man and for overall winner. Then I head back to my chair to enjoy the rest of the awards. It's the first chance I've had to really think about what the others have done. What has been achieved by a group of forty-seven people is amazing.

Paul has finished on 247km (153.5 miles), just 2km behind me and also in a strong position for GB selection.

Sarah Morwood is fifth overall and has won the prize for first woman with 213km (132.4 miles), and twenty of the forty-seven starters have run more than 100 miles. Patricia Seabrook, at the age of seventy-eight, has run 119km (73.9 miles), and eighty-five-year-old Geoff Oliver has created innumerable world records with his run of 124.4km (77.3 miles). As his result is announced, there is a collective intake of breath and by far the loudest cheer of the day. He walks across the ground where I limped minutes earlier. He is immaculate in his jacket and tie, apparently untouched by the ordeal.

Then it is over, and another chapter in the story of this special race is finished. Our community begins to disperse. Soon the track will lie empty, as if none of this has happened at all.

14:30 LIFE

Jane opens the front door and I limp inside, carrying my two trophies and a rucksack. While I sit at the bottom of the stairs trying to untie my shoelaces, she makes another few trips to the car, and soon the entrance hall is full of wet stuff. It is overwhelming and I can't begin to think how any of it will get cleared away.

I walk into the kitchen and wonder why I am there, then head back to the stairs and work my way up them, using my hands on the step in front of me to take as much of my weight as possible. It's something I did to save my legs in the days before the race, so I've had plenty of practice. I decide to shower again, now that I can use my hands and I'm not shaking. First I get a safety pin and, sitting on the edge of the bath, pierce the blood blisters on my toes, giving them a good squeeze to get the liquid out. By the time I'm finished it looks like a scene from a horror film, but the clean-up is quick and easy. The skin under my foot is loose but I decide to leave it alone.

In the shower, all the places where my skin has been chafed begin to sting. My forearms are starting to seize up from being held in position for so long during the run, and my hands and calf are swollen. But other than the calf it is all superficial, and I'm amazed to be in such good shape. After my 100-mile race I was vomiting for hours, but now I'm not feeling bad at all.

I stand in the water, enjoying its warmth. After so many hours in the wet, I feel I've earned a few minutes more. Yesterday morning I stood here wondering: *how will I feel when I stand here tomorrow?* Very good, as it turns out. And I'm proud because I did it. I actually did it.

When I'm dressed, I lower myself down the stairs, and ease into my favourite chair in the lounge. This is the moment I dreamed of for so many hours. I'm cosy and warm, and can stay here for as long as I like, not moving at all. Things get even better when Jane brings me a cup of coffee and some of my favourite biscuits. Then she brings my trophies through and puts them on the coffee table with a sandwich, water and everything else she thinks I might need. I try to explain again how grateful I am for her help and support. She is proud of what we have done but the joy of the race has subsided and the sadness has returned to her eyes. It almost breaks my heart. Then, without sitting down, she leaves to see Eve at the hospice.

The house is quiet. Sciatic pain starts to flash down my legs. My stomach aches and I know I will need to get up soon. Maybe I'll wander into my study and look at my piano, though I'm too tired to play. I'll try to think of something to eat that will meet the cravings of my body. I will eat a bit of the sandwich and then a lot of junk food that makes me feel sick. This evening, Jane will come home and I'll comfort her as she cries. And then tonight I will struggle to sleep, too uncomfortable and sore, and unable to process everything that has happened. I will lie awake, worrying and dreaming and fearing and hoping.

And then tomorrow I will go to see Eve and I will take the trophies and put them in her hands.

ACKNOWLEDGEMENTS

In order for this book to exist, there had to be a race. Thank you to my fellow athletes on the track for the smiles, nods, jokes and grimaces – it was a joy to spend those 24 hours with you. The kindness and humanity of the ultrarunning community is utterly life-affirming.

Thank you to race directors Shankara Smith and Devashishu Torpy, and to the Sri Chinmoy Marathon Team, for such a wonderful event. The enthusiastic and selfless lap counters added so much to the atmosphere of the race, and the cheerful and tireless team in the race kitchen kept the water boiling, the soup flowing and my crew defrosted and well fed. Thank you also to timekeeper Tarit Adrian Stott and race referee Ian Champion, who shared their expertise with such generosity. Carol Waugh and the medical team watched over us for many hours in appalling conditions – thank you in particular for your concern after the race.

What an amazing crew I had! Thanks to Helen Taylor for facing the twin demons of running and camping. Rob Shulman, a fine ultrarunner who could easily have been in the race himself, took his eyes off the track only to look for chocolate. Anne Wilson showed incredible powers of concentration in counting my laps, especially after the gazebo started to leak. And Toby Jacobs could be head cheerleader in any sports team.

I arrived at the track in the shape of my life, thanks to the guidance of my coach Norman Wilson. My brain was also fit for purpose, thanks to the fantastic Andy Barton, and Ann Coxon kept an eye on my physical health with the insight of the endurance swimmer she once was. The ever-positive Tara Murphy has helped me with visualisation before a number of races and I hope to carry her voice in my head for many miles to come. Thanks to my osteopath Lance Turvey for all the laughs and for getting me to the starting line in one piece. And to nutritionist Renee McGregor for understanding the role of biscuits, wine and chocolate in my regimen.

I will always be grateful to Walter Hill for introducing me to Norman and for the intelligent and motivating notes he has sent me at key moments. Thanks also to James Elson, Robbie Britton and John Pares for treating me like an athlete with promise in the months leading up to the race. And to Dan Lawson for his words in the worst of the storm.

My club, London Heathside, is a big part of my running DNA and I hope to join the great nine o'clock group more in the future. A special thanks to Sarah Swinhoe and Julian

Ferraro for that first Sunday early morning run all those years ago, and to Ed Samuel for the many final efforts up Archway Road in the cold and rain. Thanks to Asmelash Abrha for the runs in Ethiopia and London, and to Paul Jarman and Gavin Evans for setting the pace in recent times. The congratulatory note I received from club coach Jacob Howe when I was selected to run for England still means a great deal to me.

I have been fortunate to benefit from the work of some superb publishing professionals. I have learned a lot from my brilliant editor, Nick Humphrey. Nick has been incredibly generous with his support and time, and his ceaseless belief in the book has been a real gift. Thanks to my copy-editor and fellow runner Marigold Atkey for her skill and enthusiasm, and for going way above and beyond. Also to Emiliano Dacanay for the great cover design, Graeme Andrew for the brilliant typesetting, my publicist Jane Beaton for caring about whether people read this book, and my web designer Joe Cashmore for putting such intelligence and effort into my website.

A few other people provided expert encouragement at key points. Thank you Tim Adams for being so incredibly generous with your time and insights, and Matthew Lowing for your ceaseless belief in the book. And thanks to the incomparable Adharanand Finn for all the useful pointers.

My business co-founders Stuart Newstead and David Durling always listened patiently when I talked about running and writing instead of software. GB lead endurance physio Andy Walling was incredibly encouraging with his feedback. And thanks also to Angeli Mehta, Adriana Nugter, Julia Jacobs,

Melanie Orchard, Vivienne Fouche and Alvin Fun for making me feel like this was a good idea.

To Eddie Brandstatter, my best man and best friend, I am heartbroken by the sudden loss of you from my life. You brought light to everything and everyone. Melody Brandstatter, thank you for your support and friendship. Just like Eddie, you are brave, kind and amazing.

I am blessed with the positive support of these and other wonderful friends – thank you to each and every one of you.

Thank you to my family for the love and support, and for always making me feel like anything is possible.

Above all, thank you to Jane – for everything.

These are the athletes I am proud to have shared the track with: Jeff Andrews, Ann Bath, Paul Beechey, David Bone, Barney Bristow, Darren Chalk, Susie Chan, Marco Consani, Paul Corderoy, Richard Cranswick, Neil Dryland, Mylene Elliott, Tom Garrod, Roz Glover, Reima Hartikainen, Hilde Johansen, Bryn Jones, Sinead Kane, Neil Kapoor, Jens Larsson, Ingrid Lid, Gines Macia Molina, John MacLean, Lorna MacLean, Paul Maskell, Michal Masnik, Mari Mauland, Myles McCarthy, Ray McCurdy, Sarah Morwood, Bhauliya Moss, Dean Oldfield, Geoff Oliver, Timothy Rainey, Jon Regler, Brian Robb, Peter Scull, Patricia Seabrook, Tadeusz Sekretarczyk, David Shaw, Jonni Suckling, Barry Taylor, John Turner, Michael Wiggins, Nitish Zuidema, Pawel Zuk.

ABOUT THE AUTHOR

MICHAEL STOCKS has represented England and Great Britain as an ultrarunner, having made his debut for Great Britain at the age of 50. During his expansive career he has worked in corporate law, led a global organisation and founded a number of technology companies. Michael loves mountains, chocolate and playing the piano when no one is listening. He was born in South Africa, moved to the UK at the turn of the millennium, and lives in London with his wife Jane.

@michaelstocksrunner www.michael-stocks.com

Printed in Great Britain
by Amazon